GERMAN AIRCRAFT
of World War 2
in Colour

GERMAN AIRCRAFT
of World War 2
in Colour

KENNETH MUNSON

Associate RAeS

Design and Art Editor:
JOHN W. WOOD

Colour paintings:
BRIAN HILEY
JACK PELLING

Line drawings and additional research:
IAN HUNTLEY
AMRAeS

BLANDFORD PRESS
Poole   Dorset

Blandford Press Ltd
Link House, West Street,
Poole, Dorset BH15 1LL

First published 1978

Munson, Kenneth George
    German aircraft of World War II.
    1. Airplanes, Military – History
    2. World War, 1939–1945 – Aerial operations, German
    I. Title
    623.74'6'0943   UG1245.G4

ISBN 0–7137–0860–3

Set in Monophoto Plantin by Keyspools Ltd, Golborne, Lancs.
Colour reproduction & printing by Sackville Press (Billericay) Ltd, Essex
Bound by Robert Hartnoll, Bodmin, Cornwall

CONTENTS

PREFACE

THE LUFTWAFFE of Nazi Germany has acquired a mystique unrivalled by any other military air arm in aviation history, and one that is no less prevalent in the Germany of today than in those countries by whom it was opposed in 1939–1945. Created in the mid-1930s as a new arm of the Wehrmacht, it boasted nearly 4,200 front-line aircraft by the autumn of 1939; yet within six years it lay defeated, out-fought and out-bombed by superior Allied air power and starved of the fuel to continue the struggle.

The aircraft, the leaders and the operational record of Hitler's Luftwaffe have been described and dissected in countless books published since 1945, many of them highly expert and highly detailed. *German Aircraft of World War 2 in Colour 1939–1945* is, I hope, not so much a competitor to such in-depth works (several of which are listed in the Bibliography on page 159) as a more convenient 'ready reckoner' for those who require a shorter and less detailed guide to the principal Luftwaffe types of the period, and to the colours and markings that they bore. At the same time, I believe we have achieved a unique blend of artwork and photography, both colour and black and white, which presents the aircraft in a way and with an impact not previously achieved elsewhere.

The technical data are, of course, metric in origin. For English readers, linear dimensions have been converted to the nearest tenth of an inch, and areas to the nearest hundredth of a square foot; weights rounded up or down to the nearest pound; speeds rounded up or down to the nearest mile per hour, ranges to the nearest mile; and altitudes to the nearest five feet. The wing and power loadings are my own calculations, based upon these data, and are included as additional means of comparing performances. Engine ratings are, in almost every case, those at take-off.

As always, it is a particularly pleasant task to acknowledge the friends and colleagues whose efforts have made such an invaluable contribution to the finished book. Jack Wood, and artists Brian Hiley and Jack Pelling, have pulled out all the stops to make the colour artwork some of their best yet. Ian Huntley, for many years the indefatigable colour consultant and researcher for our earlier colour series, not only performed this service again but offered more tangible proof of his talents in the line drawings included. In Germany, Karl Ries remains unrivalled as a source of reference to Luftwaffe markings and unit insignia, while Hanfried Schliephake allowed generous access to his extensive library of photographs. Finally, it is a particular pleasure to welcome back Pamela Matthews, whose watchful eye and guiding hand saved one generally unfamiliar with the German language from many an unintentional *Missverständnis*.

K.M.

Seaford, Sussex,
January 1978.

PHOTOGRAPH ACKNOWLEDGEMENTS

The photographs used in this volume are from the following sources:

Air-Britain   49, 96.

Bundesarchiv   126 (top), 149 (bottom).

Dornier GmbH   39 (top), 42 (lower centre).

Bildarchiv Georg Fischbach   123 (top), 127, 148.

Focke-Wulf (VFW-Fokker)   12, 52, 63 (top), 67, 153.

Hamburger Flugzeugbau   34.

Heinkel Archiv   76 (top two and bottom), 156.

Junkers Archiv (MBB)   116, 117 (top).

Messerschmitt Archiv (MBB)   135 (bottom), 142 (bottom).

Ministry of Defence (RAE)   33 (both).

H. J. Nowarra   30, 80, 117 (lower top), 120, 133.

Archiv Schliephake   11, 15 (all), 18 (both), 20, 21, 25, 28 (both), 29, 31 (both), 35 (bottom left), 36, 39 (bottom), 42 (top two), 44, 46 (both), 51 (both), 53, 54 (both), 58 (all), 61, 63 (centre), 65 (both), 68, 70, 73 (both), 75 (both), 76 (centre), 77, 78, 82, 86, 87, 89, 90, 94, 98, 99, 102, 105, 107, 112, 114 (both), 119, 121, 123 (bottom), 126 (bottom), 128, 134, 135 (top), 138, 139, 142 (top), 149 (top), 150, 151, 152, 154, 155, 157.

US Official   13.

INTRODUCTION

There are many reasons why Germany lost the war; political, economic and military reasons which were our own fault. None of these reasons were decisive in themselves, nor were they together decisive. Had they been avoided, a more favourable development of the situation might indeed have been possible. Quite apart from them, what was decisive in itself was the loss of air supremacy.

(General Karl Koller, Chief of the Luftwaffe General Staff November 1944 to May 1945)

Since this book is concerned primarily with aircraft of the Luftwaffe between 1939–45, it is assumed that the reader has a basic acquaintance with Luftwaffe history prior to World War 2: the banning of military aircraft production by Germany in the Versailles Treaty of 1919; the gradual growth of para-military activities from the mid-1920s; the clandestine factories and flying schools in Germany and Russia; the development of high-speed 'mailplanes' and 'sporting' single-seaters that later became bombers and fighters; the open secret of the existence of a German air force following Hitler's accession to power in 1933 and the creation of the Third Reich; the official declaration of the Luftwaffe's existence two years later, on 1 March 1935; and the blooding of many of its newer combat types in the Spanish Civil War of 1936–39.

Thus prepared, in September 1939 the Luftwaffe entered World War 2 with a front-line aircraft strength of nearly 4,200 aircraft. Most of these, with the principal exception of those in reconnaissance units, were formed into Geschwadern, a Geschwader being the approximate equivalent of an RAF Group. The Geschwadern were divided into Gruppen (each Gruppe approximating to an RAF Wing), normally three in number; and

each Gruppe was in turn sub-divided into three Staffeln (Squadrons), with a usual complement of 9–12 aircraft per Staffel. Reconnaissance units were normally organised into Gruppen and Staffeln only.

With such resources, it was hardly surprising that the early months of the offensive should result in resounding successes for the German air and ground forces, which swept through Poland in less than a month, conquered Norway—with the first airborne invasion in military history—in two months, and had occupied France and the Low Countries before the end of June 1940. To Hitler and Göring, the Blitzkrieg (lightning war) doctrine had been fully vindicated. They saw no need to expand the Luftwaffe, or even to improve its existing equipment, in order to defeat Britain, and priority for aircraft production was substantially reduced. This was the first mistake, and it brought about the Luftwaffe's first serious failure.

So far, the air force had been used as a tactical weapon, creating air supremacy and providing support for the ground forces of the Wehrmacht; and it had, in the main, met little in the way of modern fighter opposition. In the spring and summer of 1940, however, its lightly-armed bombers soon proved ill-

No aircraft better typified the Luftwaffe of the early war years than the Ju 87B dive-bomber—the infamous 'Stuka'

defended against the RAF fighters, and their escorts lacked either the agility (in the case of the twin-engined Bf 110) or the range (in the case of the Bf 109) to wrest from the RAF's single-engined Hurricanes and Spitfires the air supremacy necessary for the bombers to operate unmolested. In October 1940 it was forced to switch to the night bombing of British cities—the 'Blitz'—which lasted until the spring of 1941.

Meanwhile, Hitler's pursual of his 'continental policy' in Europe and the Mediterranean resulted in the conquest of the Balkan nations and the successful invasion of Crete. Here, again because it was able to provide conditions of air supremacy against comparatively inferior opposition, the Luftwaffe's employment as a tactical air arm paid greater dividends. It was unable to reproduce that success against Malta, but was drafted in increasing numbers to North Africa following the British offensive which began in late 1941, and established a substantial strength in northern Italy, for future operations, following that country's entry into the war on 10 June 1940.

While all these operations were going on, the Luftwaffe was also playing a substantial part in the general anti-shipping war and particularly in the so-called 'Battle of the Atlantic'. Its maritime aircraft went mine-laying in the Channel and down the eastern seaboard of the British Isles; harassed and sank Allied shipping in British coastal waters, as a prelude to the proposed invasion of Britain; and partnered the U-boat submarine force in its attempts to cut off supplies to Britain from across the Atlantic and elsewhere. This anti-shipping campaign was sustained in force from the outbreak of war and was not noticeably relaxed until late 1942.

With the Luftwaffe already dispersed on several fronts, the last thing it wanted or needed—and the same was true for the other German armed services—was to be committed even further by Hitler's irrational decision to invade the Soviet Union in June 1941. Fighting on the Eastern Front made heavy demands upon Luftwaffe strength, in both men and machines, and the extensive losses suffered left it in a seriously weakened condition by the end of 1942. Nor was Russia its only problem. Already, at home, it had had to take steps to counter the nocturnal bombing of Germany in strength by the RAF, which had begun over Cologne on the night of 30/31 May 1942 with Operation

Millennium, the first 'thousand-bomber' raid. For the first time, it had had to create a night fighter force, for the bombers were becoming too numerous for comfort.

By now, airborne radar had entered the picture, both as an Allied bombing aid and as a means of helping the German night fighters to locate the enemy bombers. Daylight reprisal raids against England by fighter-bombers, and attacks by night fighter/intruders, failed materially to mitigate the Allied air offensive. By the end of 1942 the Luftwaffe had to face the facts that its strategies had been wrong; that its future policy was, to say the least, indecisive; and that it was going to have to prepare to fight a much longer war than at first anticipated. Aircraft production was stepped up, and fresh looks were taken at designs to replace or improve upon the aircraft already in service. The situation worsened in 1943 with the addition of USAAF day bombers to the attack on Germany, to provide a round-the-clock bombing offensive with the RAF, and with the failure of the Luftwaffe in Russia. This decline in the Luftwaffe's fortunes

came to a head on 18 August 1943, following a particularly devastating attack by the RAF on the rocket testing centre at Peenemünde, when Generaloberst Hans Jeschonnek, Chief of the Luftwaffe General Staff, committed suicide.

Jeschonnek's successor, General Günther Korten, started with the right idea. He reorganised the Luftwaffe giving priority to strategic bombing, especially of Russia, and to home defence, reducing the use of air power in support of the Army to a minimum. Unfortunately for Korten's plans, the Russian counter-offensive between the summer of 1943 and the spring of 1944 largely negated the strategic bombing of Russian targets. Meanwhile, the Axis powers had been driven out of North Africa and the Allies were advancing steadily upward through Italy.

Nevertheless, during the first half of 1944 Korten had some cause for optimism. His first-line aircraft strength was now in excess of 5,500; the fuel situation (which had been something of a problem) was beginning to show signs of improvement; and so was the supply of better-trained aircrew from the flying schools. Several long-awaited newer

Maritime marauder of the Battle of the Atlantic—the aptly-named Condor (Fw 200), which helped the U-boats to prey upon Allied shipping

GERMAN AIRCRAFT PRODUCTION

3 September 1939 to 8 May 1945

	1939	1940	1941	1942	1943	1944	1945	Totals
Bombers	737	2,852	3,373	4,337	4,649	2,287	—	18,235
Fighters	605	2,746	3,744	5,515	10,898	25,285	4,935	53,728
Ground Attack	134	603	507	1,249	3,266	5,496	1,104	12,359
Reconnaissance	163	971	1,079	1,067	1,117	1,686	216	6,299
Seaplanes	100	269	183	238	259	141	—	1,190
Transports	145	388	502	573	1,028	443	—	3,079
Gliders	—	378	1,461	745	442	111	8	3,145
Communications	46	170	431	607	874	410	11	2,549
Trainers	588	1,870	1,121	1,078	2,274	3,693	318	10,942
Jet Aircraft	—	—	—	—	—	1,041	947	1,988
Totals	2,518	10,247	12,401	15,409	24,807	40,593	7,539	113,514

types of aircraft were starting to enter service, such as the He 177 and Ju 188 bombers, the Me 410 Zerstörer and the He 219 night fighter; much was expected of the new generation of jet fighters then under development; and the night fighter force was beginning to be effective against the Allied bombers.

Two main factors were to conspire against his optimism. First, since the early summer of 1943 the Allied bombing offensive had been concentrated more and more against the centres of German aircraft and aero-engine production (see map on page 145); second, the appearance of American day fighters such as the long-range Mustang,

A wartime assembly line of Focke-Wulf Fw 190 single-seat fighters

An abandoned Me 262A jet fighter-bomber, found by the US Army in a wood near Frankfurt in the spring of 1945. A 250 kg bomb and some 30 mm ammunition lie on the ground under the wings, together with parts of the engine cowlings; but the jet engines have been removed to avoid capture

which provided much-needed protection to the previously unescorted USAAF day bombers penetrating deep into Reich territory. (It has been estimated that Allied raids between mid-1943 and the end of 1944 cost the Luftwaffe some 14,000 fighters and 4,000 other types in lost production. On the other hand, if these aircraft *had* been received, shortages of aircrew, fuel and munitions would have severely limited their effective use.) Added to this campaign were specific Allied attacks on Romanian and other oilfields producing fuel for the German war effort.

Then, in the summer of 1944, came the D-day landings in France and the Russian advance into Poland, and from then on the decline gathered momentum. Panic measures, such as the V-weapons programme, the expansion of fighter production to the virtual exclusion of bombers and other types (see the table on page 12), the advent of jet- and rocket-powered interceptors, all came too late to stem the tide. The night fighter force declined in effectiveness; the concerted attack on Allied airfields in Europe at the beginning of 1945—Operation Bodenplatte—failed; and, eventually, the fuel ran out.

In August 1939, on the eve of war, Göring's Order of the Day to the Luftwaffe had spoken of an air force "inspired by faith in our Führer and Commander-in-Chief . . . ready to carry out every command of the Führer with lightning speed and undreamed-of might". The reality, the epitaph for an air force that was failed by its masters, was written after the war by General Karl Koller, who succeeded to the position of Chief of the Luftwaffe General Staff after the death of General Korten:

"We remained voices crying in vain in the wilderness. Promises were made to build up the largest air force possible after the close of the Russian war. Millions of soldiers were then to be released from the Army and were to be sent to the aircraft industry and to the German Air Force. Only the Air Force was to be built up. In the meanwhile, however, the air armament was put way down on the list; first were submarines, then came tanks, then assault guns, then howitzers or Lord knows what, and then came the Air Force. Meanwhile, the Russian war was eating away men, material, armament and planes and the only thing that remained for the Air Force was a promise that was never kept. Its task was to make sacrifices."

LUFTWAFFE UNIT CODES

Letter/numeral combinations were adopted, except on fighters, to identify the unit to which an aircraft belonged. They appeared on the fuselage, to the left of the national marking, with aircraft and Staffel identity letters to the right.

A1 Kampfgeschwader 53 'Legion Condor'.
A2 I./Zerstörergeschwader 52 (retained after re-designation as II./Zerstörergeschwader 2 on 6 July 1940).
A3 Kampfgeschwader 200.
A5 I./Stukageschwader 1 (and, possibly, other Gruppen of St.G.1; retained after redesignation as Schlachtgeschwader 1).
A6 Aufklärungsgruppe 120.

B3 Kampfgeschwader 54 'Totenkopf' (from mid-March 1940).
B4 Stab. flight of unidentified Nachtjagddivision.

C1 Erprobungsstelle Peenemünde (also known as Erprobungskommando 16).
C2 Aufklärungsgruppe 41.
C6 Kampfgeschwader zur besonderen Verwendung 600.
C8 Transportgeschwader 5.
C9 Nachtjagdgeschwader 5.

D1 Seeaufklärungsgruppe 126.
D5 Nachtjagdgeschwader 3.
D9 Nachtjagdstaffel Finnland/Norwegen.

E1
E2
E3
E4 } Erprobungsstelle Rechlin.
E5
E6
E7

F1 Kampfgeschwader 76 (also I./Stukageschwader 76, retained also after its redesignation as III./Stukageschwader 77).
F2 Ergänzungs (Fern) Gruppe.
F6 Aufklärungsgruppe 122.
F7 Seeaufklärungsgruppe 130.
F8 Kampfgeschwader 40.

G1 Kampfgeschwader 55 'Griefen'.
G2 Aufklärungsgruppe 124.
G6 Kampfgeschwader zur besonderen Verwendung 2 (also, later, Transportgeschwader 4).
G9 Zerstörergeschwader 1 'Wespen' (also, later, Nachtjagdgeschwader 1 and Nachtjagdgeschwader 4).

H1 Aufklärungsgruppe 12.
H4 Luftlandegeschwader 1.

H7 Stukageschwader 3.
H8 Aufklärungsgruppe 33.

J2 Nahaufklärungsgruppe 3.
J4 Junkers 290 Staffel (later, Transportstaffel 5).
J9 I. (Stuka)/Trägergruppe 186 'Graf Zeppelin' (retained after redesignation as III./Stukageschwader 1 on 6 July 1940; also Stukageschwader 5).

K1 Stab. flight of Luftflotte 6.
K6 Küstenfliegergruppe 406.
K7 Aufklärungsgruppe Nacht.
K9★ Aufklärungsgruppe Oberbefehlshaber der Luftwaffe.

L1 Lehrgeschwader 1.
L2 Lehrgeschwader 2.
L5 Kampfgruppe zur besonderen Verwendung 5.

M2 Küstenfliegergruppe 106.
M7 Kampfgruppe 806.
M8 I. and II./Zerstörergeschwader 76.

N3★ Kampfgeschwader zur besonderen Verwendung 172.

P1 Kampfgeschwader 60.
P2 Aufklarüngsgruppe 21.
P4 Korps Kette Führungskette X. Fliegerkorps.
P5 Sonderstaffel 'Trans-Ozean'.

R4 I. and II./Nachtjagdgeschwader 2.

S1 Stukageschwader 3.
S2 Stukageschwader 77 (also Schlachtgeschwader 77).
S3 Transportgruppe 30.
S4 Küstenfliegergruppe 506.
S7 Stukageschwader 3 (also Schlachtgeschwader 3).
S9 Erprobungsgruppe 210 (later Schnellkampfgeschwader 210; also Zerstörergeschwader 1).

T1 Aufklärungsgruppe 10 'Tannenberg'.
T3 Bordfliegergruppe 196.
T5 Aufklärungsgruppe Oberbefehlshaber der Luftwaffe (later Aufklärungsgruppe 100; also Wettererkundungsstaffel Oberbefehlshaber der Luftwaffe as T5 + .. U).
T6 Stukageschwader 2 'Immelmann' (also Schlachtgeschwader 2; also Stuka Ergänzungsstaffel of VIII. Fliegerkorps as T6 + .. Z).

T9 Versuchsverband Oberbefehlshaber der Luftwaffe (later redesignated Oberkommando der Luftwaffe; also various Sonderkommando).

U5 Kampfgeschwader 2 'Holzhammer'.
U8 I./Zerstörergeschwader 26 'Horst Wessel' (until June 1941).

V4 Kampfgeschwader 1 'Hindenburg'.
V7 Aufklärungsgruppe 32.
V8 Nachtschlachtgruppe 1.

W1
W2
W3 Reserved for use by Messerschmitt Me 321
W4 Gigant units.
W5
W6
W7 Nachtjagdgeschwader 100.
W8 Reserved for use by Messerschmitt Me 321 Gigant units.
W9 Reserved for use by Messerschmitt Me 323 units.

X4 Lufttransportstaffel (See) 222 (later redesignated Seeaufklärungsgruppe 129).

Z6 I./Kampfgeschwader 66.

1A Wettererkundungsstaffel 5.
1B Wettererkundungsstaffel 5 (as 1B + .. H).
1B 13.(Z)/Jagdgeschwader 5 'Eismeer' (as 1B + .. X).
1G Kampfgeschwader 27 'Boelcke'.
1H Kampfgeschwader 26 'Löwen'.
1K Nachtschlachtgruppe 4.
1R Unidentified Kurier Staffel based in Finland.
1T Kampfgruppe 126 (later Kampfgeschwader 28).
1Z Kampfgeschwader zur besonderen Verwendung 1 (later redesignated Transportgeschwader 1).

2F Kampfgeschwader 54 'Totenkopf' (until mid-March 1940).
2H Versuchsstaffel 210.
2J Zerstörergeschwader 1 'Wespen'.
2N II./Zerstörergeschwader 1 'Wespen' (redesignated III./Zerstörergeschwader 76 in July 1940).
2P X. Fliegerdivision.
2S Zerstörergeschwader 2.
2Z Nachtjagdgeschwader 6 (from 1 August 1943).

3C Nachtjagdgeschwader 4 (also, from 1 January–30 July 1943, Nachtjagdgeschwader 5).
3E Kampfgeschwader 6.
3J* Nachtjagdgeschwader 3.
3K Minensuchgruppe der Luftwaffe.
3M I./Zerstörergeschwader 2.
3U Zerstörergeschwader 26 'Horst Wessel' (from

July 1941; also, later, liaison aircraft of Jagdgeschwader 6).
3W Nachtschlachtgruppe 11.
3X* I./Kampfgeschwader 152 (later redesignated II./Kampfgeschwader 1).
3Z Kampfgeschwader 153 (later, Kampfgeschwader 77).

4A IV./Zerstörergeschwader 26 'Horst Wessel'.
4D I./Kampfgeschwader 25 (also Kampfgeschwader 30 'Adler').
4E Aufklärungsgruppe 13 (also, later, Nahaufklärungsgruppe 15).
4M* Aufklärungsgruppe 11.
4N Aufklärungsgruppe 22.
4R Nachtjagdgeschwader 2 (some units only).
4T Wettererkundungsstaffel 51.
4U Aufklärungsgruppe 123.
4V Kampfgeschwader zur besonderen Verwendung 172 (also, Transportgeschwader 3 and some aircraft of Transportgeschwader 4).

5D Aufklärungsgruppe 31.
5F Aufklärungsgruppe 14 (also, later, Nahaufklärungsgruppe 14).
5J Kampfgeschwader 4 'General Wever'.
5K Kampfgeschwader 3 'Blitz'.
5M Aufklärungsgruppe 122.
5T Kampfschulgeschwader 1 (later redesignated Kampfgeschwader 101 from 1 February 1943; also used by an unidentified reconnaissance unit).
5Z Wettererkundungsstaffel 26.

6G III./Stukageschwader 51 (later redesignated II./Stukageschwader 1 from 6 July 1940).
6I Küstenfliegergruppe 706.
6K Aufklärungsgruppe 41.
6M Aufklärungsgruppe 11 (also Küstenstaffel 'Krim' and, later, some aircraft of Nahaufklärungsgruppe 8).
6N Kampfgruppe 100 (later redesignated Kampfgeschwader 100).
6R Seeaufklärungsgruppe 127.
6U Zerstörergeschwader 1 'Wespen'.
6W Bordfliegergruppe 196 (also, later, Seeaufklärungsgruppe 128).
6Z Gruppe Herzog.

7A Aufklärungsgruppe 121.
7J Nachtjagdgeschwader 102.
7R Seeaufklärungsgruppe 125.
7T Küstenfliegergruppe 606.
7U Kampfgruppe zur besonderen Verwendung 108.
7V Kampfgruppe zur besonderen Verwendung 700.

8H Aufklärungsgruppe 33.
8L Küstenfliegergruppe 906.
8T Kampfgruppe zur besonderen Verwendung 800 (also, later, Transportgeschwader 2).
8V Nachtjagdgeschwader 200.

9K Kampfgeschwader 51 'Edelweiss'.
9P Kampfgruppe zur besonderen Verwendung 9.
9V Fernaufklärungsgruppe 5.
9W Nachtjagdgeschwader 101.

* Not confirmed.

Arado Ar 66C two-seat trainer

ARADO Ar 66

Developed by Dipl-Ing Walter Blume from an original 1931 design by Walter Rethel, the Ar 66 was among the first standard Luftwaffe training aircraft. The Ar 66a first prototype flew at Brandenburg-Neuendorf in 1932, and was followed by an Ar 66b prototype and 10 production Ar 66B seaplanes with twin wooden floats and an enlarged rudder. A third (Ar 66c) prototype, generally similar to the Ar 66a, followed; and the production version of this, designated Ar 66C, was delivered from 1933. In addition to Arado production, contracts were placed in 1935 with BFW (for 90) and the Gothaer Waggonfabrik. The Ar 66C still equipped a small number of FFS during the early years of World War 2. Its wartime career also included service with several Luftwaffe harassment squadrons (Störkampfstaffeln) in Finland, Latvia and the USSR, when, together with the Gotha Go 145, it was used for nocturnal nuisance raids behind the Soviet lines with 2 kg or 4 kg anti-personnel bombs. *Data : page 146.*

ARADO Ar 68 and Ar 197

This single-seat fighter was designed in 1933 to succeed the Heinkel He 51. Five prototypes were built, the Ar 68a (D-IKIN) and Ar 68d (D-ITAR) each having a 750 hp BMW VId engine; the Ar 68b (D-IVUS) and Ar 68c (D-IBAS) a 610 hp supercharged Junkers Jumo 210; and the Ar 68e (D-ITEP) a 680 hp Jumo 210Da. First flight, by the Ar 68a at Warnemünde in the early

Arado Ar 68F-1, with BMW VI engine

Arado Ar 197 V3 production prototype

LUFTWAFFE COLOURS

To reduce the possibility of misinterpreting the colour plates which follow, the official RLM colour number is cross-referenced to two internationally accepted colour 'dictionaries': first, the Methuen *Handbook of Colour*, then (in brackets) to the US publication *Colours* (Federal Standard F.S.595a). An asterisk indicates an approximate match only. The values given are typical averages: it will be appreciated that each falls within an 'envelope' of darker or lighter tones, depending upon age and operational conditions. Most Luftwaffe exterior colours gave a matt, silky finish with a slight sheen, particularly after some service use. For this reason, 'semi-gloss' references have been quoted for the F.S.595a values.

RLM 00	RLM 01	RLM 02	RLM 03	RLM 04	RLM 21
wasserhell	silber	RLM-grau	silber	gelb	weiss
(transparent)	(silver)	(RLM grey)	(silver)	(yellow)	(white)
		27 D/E 2		4 B 8	
—	—		—		
—	(17178)	(24159–34226)	—	(23538)	(27780)

RLM 22	RLM 23	RLM 24	RLM 25	RLM 26	RLM 27	RLM 28
schwarz	rot	dunkelblau	hellgrün	braun	gelb	weinrot
(black)	(red)	(dark blue)	light green	(brown)	(yellow)	(ruby)
—	9 A/B 8	21 E/F 7	26 D 6/7	7 E/F 7/8	3C 7/8	11 F/G 8
(27038)	(21302)	*(25053)	(24115)	(20091)	*(23481)	*(20049–21136)

†RLM 61	†RLM 62	†RLM 63	RLM 65	RLM 66	RLM 70	RLM 71
dunkelbraun	grün	hellgrau	hellblau	schwarzgrau	schwarzgrün	dunkelgrün
(dark brown)	(green)	(light grey)	(light blue)	(black-grey)	(black-green)	(dark green)
6 F/G 4/5	27 E/F 3	1/2 B/C 2	*24 B 2/3	21 F 1	28 G 2	29/30 F 3
(20045–30099)	(24128)	(26400–26559)	(25622–25414)	(26081)	(24052)	(24079)

‡RLM 72	‡RLM 73	RLM 74	RLM 75	RLM 76	RLM 77	¶RLM 78
grün	grün	dunkelgrau	grau	weissblau	hellgrau	himmelblau
(green)	(green)	(dark grey)	(grey)	(white-blue)	(light grey)	(sky blue)
26 F 3	26 G 3	26 F 2	22 F 2	23/24 A 2	30 C 1/2	*23 B 4
(24056)	*(24077)	(26081)	(26118)	(25622)	(26408)	(25414)

¶RLM 79	¶RLM 79	¶RLM 80	¶RLM 80	§RLM 81	§RLM 82	RLM 82
sandgelb	sandgelb	olivgrün	olivgrün	dunkelgrün	grün	grün
(sand yellow)	(sand yellow)	(olive green)	(olive green)	(dark green)	(green)	(green)
4/5 D 6	*or* 6/7 C/D 4	4 F/G 8 *or*	29 F 6	3/4 F 3	26/27 E 8 *or*	28 F 4
(20257)	*or* (20227–20313)	*(20118–24087) *or*	(24102)	(24091–24087)	(24110) *or*	(24906)

† *Discontinued gradually from 1938 ; a few older types only remained in these colours up to about the end of 1941.*
‡ *Maritime aircraft.*
¶ *North Africa and Mediterranean.*
§ *Home Defence from 1943.*

summer of 1934, revealed below-par performance, and it was planned to adopt the Jumo engine as standard. However, the Ar 68F-1 (750 hp BMW VI 7·3Z) was first into production. Deliveries began in the late summer of 1936, but relatively few had been completed before this was supplanted in the autumn by the main production version, the Ar 68E-1. Armed with two MG 17 machine-guns in the upper cowling, the Ar 68E-1 had provision for six 10 kg SC 10 bombs under the fuselage. The Ar 68G (BMW high-altitude engine) was not built; an Ar 68H prototype (D-ISIX), with an 850 hp super-charged BMW 132Da, enclosed cockpit and two extra MG 17s (in the upper wing), exhibited better performance but did not enter production. Several Ar 68E-1s served with 10. and 11. (Nachtjagd)/JG 72, and a few Ar 68F-1s with 10. (Nachtjagd)/JG 53, during the early months of the war; but by then most had become advanced trainers with the Jagdfliegerschulen. The Ar 197 was developed as a carrier fighter-bomber, the V1 (D-ITSE) flying in early 1937 with a 960 hp DB 600A engine. The V2 (D-IVLE, with 815 hp BMW 132J) and V3 (880 hp BMW 132Dc) were test-flown at Travemünde the same year, the latter having two MG 17s in the cowling, two 20 mm MG FF cannon in the top wing, provision for four underwing 50 kg SC 50 bombs and an under-fuselage fuel tank or smoke canister; but by the end of 1937 the Ar 197 programme had been abandoned. *Data: page 146.*

ARADO Ar 95 and Ar 195

The first of five Ar 95 torpedo/bomber/reconnaissance prototypes (D-OLUO) flew in autumn 1936. The Luftwaffe's two-seat Ar 95A-1 served until 1944 with SAGr 125, 126 or 127, mainly around the Baltic Sea. It could carry either a 700 kg torpedo or one 375 kg and six 50 kg bombs, and was armed with a 7·9 mm MG 17 fixed gun forward and a movable 7·9 mm MG 15 in the rear cockpit. The three prototype Ar 195s competed unsuccessfully in 1938 with the Fieseler Fi 167. *Data: page 146.*

ARADO Ar 96 and Ar 396

A production total of 11,546 testifies to the importance of the Ar 96, which was the principal advanced trainer at the Luftwaffe's wartime flying schools. Many others were employed for reconnaissance, liaison and communications by various other units. First flown in 1938, the Ar 96 V1 (D-IRUU) had a 240 hp Argus As 10C-3 engine, which also powered the few Ar 96A-1s which entered service from the spring of 1939. Main production, by Arado and AGO in Germany and later by Avia and Letov in Czechoslovakia,

Arado Ar 95A-1 two-seat torpedo bomber

Arado Ar 195 V1 first prototype **(D-OCLN)**

Aircraft type		Ar 96B-2
Power plant		1 × 465 hp As 410A-1
Accommodation		2
Wing span	m : ft in	11·00 : 36 1·1
Length overall	m : ft in	9·13 : 29 11·4
Height overall	m : ft in	2·64 : 8 7·9
Wing area	m² : sq ft	17·10 : 184·06
Weight empty	kg : lb	1,295 : 2,855
Weight loaded	kg : lb	1,695 : 3,737
Max wing loading	kg/m² : lb/sq ft	99·12 : 20·30
Max power loading	kg/hp : lb/hp	3·64 : 8·04
Max level speed	km h : mph	330 : 205
at (height)	m : ft	3,000 : 9,845
Cruising speed	km h : mph	295 : 183
at (height)	m : ft	3,000 : 9,845
Time to 3,000 m (9,845 ft)		6·8 min
Service ceiling	m : ft	7,100 : 23,295
Range (normal)	km : miles	990 : 615

centred upon the Ar 96B series, variants of which included the unarmed B-1 pilot trainer, the B-2 gunnery trainer (7·9mm MG 17 in the front fuselage), and the B-5 (an improved B-2). Some Ar 96Bs were fitted with two underwing MG 17 guns; some were supplied to Hungary (35) and Romania.

A mixed-construction development, the Ar 396, flew on 29 December 1944 with a 580 hp As 411 MA-1, new dual-control cockpits and semi-retractable landing gear. Only a few prototypes, by SIPA in France and Letov, were completed during the war.

Arado Ar 96B-5 of an unidentified Jagdfliegerschule, *ca* 1943

| 02 | 04 | 21 | 22 | 65 | 70 |

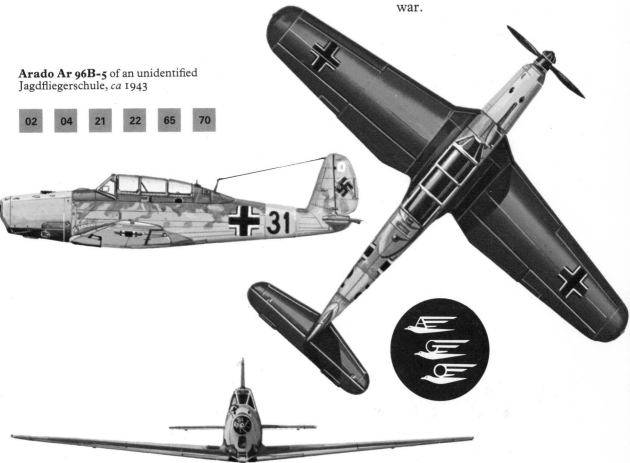

Arado Ar 196A-3 (7R + BK) of 2./SAGr 125, Aegean theatre, winter 1941/42

Staffel emblem of **2./SAGr 125**

Aircraft type		Ar 196A-3
Power plant		1 × 960 hp BMW 132K
Accommodation		2
Wing span	m : ft in	12·44 : 40 9·8
Length overall	m : ft in	11·00 : 36 1·1
Height overall	m : ft in	4·45 : 14 7·2
Wing area	m² : sq ft	28·35 : 305·16
Weight empty	kg : lb	2,577 : 5,681
Weight loaded	kg : lb	3,310 : 7,297
Wing loading	kg/m² : lb/sq ft	116·75 : 23·91
Power loading	kg/hp : lb/hp	3·45 : 7·60
Max level speed	km/h : mph	312 : 194
at (height)	m : ft	4,000 : 13,125
Cruising speed	km/h : mph	253 : 157
at (height)	m : ft	— : —
S/L rate of climb	m/min : ft/min	300 : 984
Service ceiling	m : ft	7,000 : 22,965
Range	km : miles	*800 : 497

* at 253 km/h (157 mph)

Arado Ar 196A-2 (BB + YC) twin-float seaplane on its beaching trolley

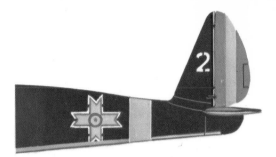

Bulgarian Air Force markings (No. 161 Squadron) on an **Ar 196A-3**, *ca* 1943

Romanian Air Force markings (No. 102 Squadron) on an **Ar 196A-3**, spring 1944

ARADO Ar 196

This maritime reconnaissance, patrol and attack seaplane, designed in 1936 to replace the Heinkel He 60, first flew in mid-1937, the Ar 196 V1 (D-IEHK) and V2 both being of twin-float configuration. Three additional prototypes and a small number of pre-production Ar 196B-0s were built later with a central main float and twin outboard stabilising floats, but the main Ar 196A production series followed the twin-float arrangement. Ten pre-production Ar 196A-0s were followed by 20 A-1s and a total of 506 A-3, A-4 and A-5 models, this total including 23 A-3s by SNCASO at St Nazaire in France and 69 A-5s by Fokker in the Netherlands.

The Ar 196A entered service in late 1938 and during the war served under Bord-fliegergruppe 196 on board the major German warships *Admiral Graf Spee*, *Admiral Scheer*, *Bismarck*, *Gneisenau*, *Lützow*, *Prinz Eugen*, *Scharnhorst* and *Tirpitz*; and with seven SAGr (Seeaufklärungsgruppen), KG 100 and 200, and Küstenfliegergruppe 706, from coastal bases in virtually every European, Mediterranean and Balkan theatre of operations. All except the Ar 196A-5 (which had an MG81Z twin gun) mounted a single movable 7·9mm MG15 gun in the rear cockpit; the A-2 to A-5 had also a cowling-mounted MG17 and two wing-mounted 20mm MG FF cannon; all models had provision for carrying a 50kg bomb beneath each wing.

Right: A fully dismantled **Ar 231**, with wings and floats stowed alongside the fuselage within a 2·00 m (6 ft 6·7 in) diameter tubular 'hangar' for carriage on board a submarine

Below: Side elevation of the **Arado Ar 231** single-seat observation seaplane

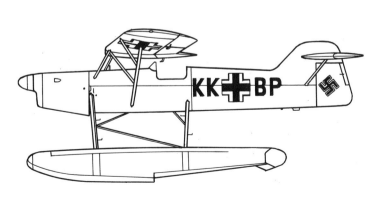

ARADO Ar 231

Although it was never operational, the Ar 231 was an ingenious design resurrecting the concept of an observation seaplane small enough to be carried by a submarine to spot for enemy convoys and warships. It was designed in 1940, and the first of six prototypes (V1 to V6) flew early in the following year. It could be rigged and launched, or retrieved and stowed, in about six minutes, the floats being detached and the wings folding back across the fuselage; the aircraft then fitted into a 2·00m diameter storage tube. However, trials revealed several unsatisfactory handling qualities; moreover, U-boat commanders were, understandably, reluctant to linger on the surface while it was launched or retrieved, and the Ar 231 was abandoned in early 1942 in favour of the Focke-Achgelis Fa 330. *Data : page 146.*

Arado Ar 232 V2 (VD + YB) in typical mid-war camouflage scheme. This aircraft was used by the Luftwaffe in the winter of 1942/43 to support the 6th Army at Stalingrad, and later by the Arado-Staffel of the Ergänzungs-Transport Gruppe

ARADO Ar 232

One of several attempts to evolve a successor to the Junkers Ju 52/3m, the Arado Ar 232 was designed to a 1939 RLM specification and flew for the first time in the early summer of 1941. The V1 and V2 prototypes were each powered, as specified, by two 1,600 hp BMW 801MA engines, but the Ar 232A production model based on them was abandoned when priority for the supply of these engines was needed by the Fw 190 fighter programme. Development therefore continued with the Ar 232B series, whose V3 (B-01) prototype was flown in May 1942. This differed mainly in having a 1·70 m (5 ft 6·9in) increase in wing span, to accommodate four BMW-Bramo 323R-2 engines. Of distinctive layout, the Ar 232B featured a pod-and-boom fuselage, with a hydraulically operated rear-loading door; a retractable tricycle landing gear; and a row of ten pairs of small idler wheels (11 pairs on the V1/V2) under the fuselage centreline, on to which the aircraft could sink to lower the cabin floor to truck-bed height for the loading of vehicles, troops or equipment. A dorsal turret aft of the flight deck mounted a 20 mm MG 151/20 cannon, and there were single movable 13 mm machine-guns in the nose and above the rear-loading door. This armament could be supplemented, if required, by up to eight 7·9 mm MG 34 infantry machine-guns firing through the side windows. Eight pre-production Ar 232B-0s (V4–V11) are known to have been built, though 10 more B-series aircraft were ordered. Arado retained one as a testbed (and later as supply transport for the Ar 234 programme); most of the others (including the V1 and V2) were assigned to Luftwaffe transport or special-duty units on the Eastern Front from the winter of 1942–43. Two (the V8/B-05 and V11/B-08) served with Wekusta 5 in Norway, the latter having a non-retractable ski undercarriage and the former a powerplant of four 700 hp Gnome-Rhône 14M radial engines.

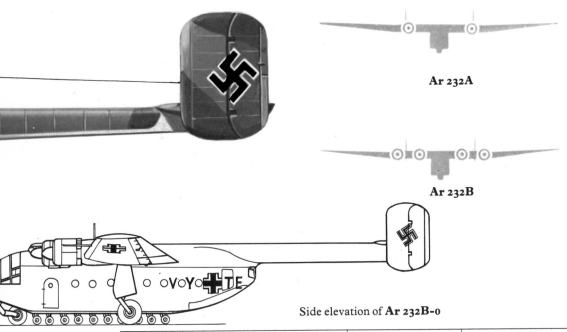

Ar 232A

Ar 232B

Side elevation of **Ar 232B-0**

Aircraft type			Ar 232 V1	Ar 232B-0
Power plant			2 × 1,600 hp BMW 801MA	4 × 1,200 hp BMW-Bramo 323R-2
Accommodation			4 + cargo	4 + cargo
Wing span	m	: ft in	21·80 : 71 6·3	33·50 : 109 10·9
Length overall	m	: ft in	23·52 : 77 2·0	23·52 : 77 2·0
Height overall	m	: ft in	5·70 : 18 8·4	5·70 : 18 8·4
Wing area	m²	: sq ft	— : —	142·60 : 1,534·93
Weight empty	kg	: lb	16,600 : 36,597	12,780 : 28,175
Weight loaded	kg	: lb	21,130 : 46,584	20,000 : 44,092
Max wing loading	kg/m²	: lb/sq ft	— : —	140·25 : 13·03
Max power loading	kg/hp	: lb/hp	6·60 : 14·56	5·00 : 11·02
Max level speed	km/h	: mph	338 : 210	308 : 191
at (height)	m	: ft	5,500 : 18,045	4,000 : 13,125
Cruising speed	km/h	: mph	— : —	288 : 179
at (height)	m	: ft	— : —	2,000 : 6,560
Time to 2,000 m (6,560 ft)			—	7 min
Service ceiling	m	: ft	— : —	6,900 : 22,640
Range	km	: miles	— : —	1,335 : 830

21
22
65
70
71

**Arado Ar 240A-02 (V6) (GL + QF) of
13.(Z)/JG 5 'Eismeer'**, northern Finland,
winter 1942/43

Arado Ar 234 V1 on its take-off trolley

ARADO Ar 234 BLITZ (Lightning)

This clean and attractive twin-jet aircraft's design
started in late 1940, around a pair of 840 kg
(1,852 lb) st Jumo 004A turbojets, but through
delays in engine development the Ar 234 V1—first
of 40 Versuchs machines eventually ordered—did
not fly until 15 June 1943. The V3 had a pressurised
cabin, ejection seats and Walter assisted take-off
rockets, and the V5 was powered by 900 kg
(1,984 lb) st BMW 003As for comparison. The intended Ar 234A production series was abandoned
after trials with a jettisonable take-off trolley; skids
beneath the engine and fuselage were provided for

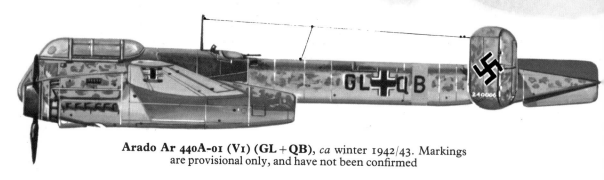

Arado Ar 440A-01 (V1) (GL + QB), *ca* winter 1942/43. Markings
are provisional only, and have not been confirmed

24

04	21
22	23
27	63
65	70
71	75
77	

Arado Ar 234B-2 (F1 + AS) of 8./KG 76, Laerz, January 1945

Arado Ar 234C-3 (four BMW 003A-1 engines)

landing. The first production version was therefore the Ar 234B, based on the V9. First flown on 10 March 1944, this had retractable tricycle landing gear. After small numbers of the Ar 234B-0 and B-1 for unarmed reconnaissance, which entered service in July 1944, the Ar 234B-2 was the first production bomber—the first in the world with turbojet power. It entered service in late 1944 with KG 76, and could carry a bomb load of 1,500 kg (3,307 lb); some aircraft were armed with two rearward-firing 20 mm MG 151 cannon in the lower aft fuselage. By this time the Blitz enjoyed a high production priority, and 210 Ar 234 B-1/B-2s were built, but due to accidents in training (mostly because the techniques of handling jet aircraft were unfamiliar) comparatively few became operational. Their employment during 1944–45 was primarily for reconnaissance over the UK and northern Italy, or for bombing over the Western Front, notably during the Ardennes offensive and the Rhine crossing in the spring of 1945. The next production model, the Ar 234C, was a multi-purpose series with four 800 kg (1,764 lb) st BMW 003A-1 engines. The C-1 was intended for reconnaissance, the C-2 for bombing, and the C-3 for bombing, ground attack (with anti-personnel bombs) or night fighting (with two additional MG 151s in a forward-firing ventral pack), but only 14 C-1/C-3s were completed. Further C variants, for reconnaissance, night fighting or bombing, were under development in the spring of 1945, and 10 prototypes had been started for the Ar 234D, to be powered by two Heinkel Hirth HeS 011A turbojets. Other projects included the Ar 234E (a Zerstörer variant of the D), Ar 234F, Ar 234P night fighter and rocket-powered Ar 234R.

ARADO Ar 240 and Ar 440

This advanced multi-purpose warplane first flew on 10 May 1940, but soon revealed serious instability problems which subsequent re-design failed to eliminate. Only 15 (the Ar 240 V1 to V4, five A-os, two B-os and four C-os) were completed, and only six of these saw operational service. They were the V3, evaluated by the Aufklärungsgruppe ob d L in mid-1941, and the five AGO-built pre-production Ar 240A-os. The latter were issued in 1943, initially to JG 5 in Finland (two), 1. and 3.(F)/100 on the Eastern Front (one each), and 1.(F)/123 in Italy (one). Armament provision was made for one dorsal and one ventral remotely controlled barbette, each mounting 7·9 mm MG 81Z twin guns, plus two 7·9 mm MG 17 guns in the nose. The Ar 440 was a much-redesigned development, with a planned armament of two 13 mm MG 131s, three 20 mm MG 151s and two 30 mm MK 108 cannon, plus a 1,000 kg (2,205 lb) bomb load. First flown in early summer 1942, it proved far superior to the Ar 240; but production was eventually rejected in favour of the Dornier Do 335, and only four were completed.

Aircraft type		Ar 234B-2	Ar 240A-0	Ar 440A-0
Power plant		2 × 900 kg (1,984 lb) st Jumo 004B	2 × 1,175 hp DB 601E	2 × 1,900 hp DB 603G
Accommodation		1	2	2
Wing span	m : ft in	14·11 : 46 3·5	13·335 : 43 9·0	16·27 : 53 4·6
Length overall	m : ft in	12·64 : 41 5·6	12·81 : 42 0·3	14·28 : 46 10·2
Height overall	m : ft in	4·30 : 14 1·3	3·95 : 12 11·5	4·00 : 13 1·5
Wing area	m² : sq ft	26·40 : 284·17	31·30 : 336·91	35·00 : 376·74
Weight empty	kg : lb	5,200 : 11,464	6,200 : 13,669	9,200 : 20,282
Weight loaded	kg : lb	***9,850 : 21,715	9,450 : 20,834	12,200 : 26,896
Max wing loading	kg/m² : lb/sq ft	373·11 : 76·42	301·92 : 61·84	348·57 : 71·39
Max power loading	kg/hp or lb/hp or kg/kg st : lb/lb st	5·47 : 5·47	4·38 : 9·66	3·91 : 8·62
Max level speed	km/h : mph	****742 : 461	618 : 384	**752 : 467
at (height)	m : ft	6,000 : 19,685	6,000 : 19,685	11,200 : 36,745
Cruising speed	km/h : mph	— : —	555 : 345	— : —
at (height)	m : ft	— : —	6,000 : 19,685	— : —
Time to 6,000 m (19,685 ft)		—	11·0 min	—
Service ceiling	m : ft	10,000 : 32,810	10,500 : 34,450	— : —
Range	km : miles	*1,100 : 684	2,000 : 1,243	***2,700 : 1,678

* with 1,500 kg (3,307 lb) bomb load   ** with GM 1 boost   *** maximum   **** in clean condition

BACHEM Ba 349 NATTER (Viper)

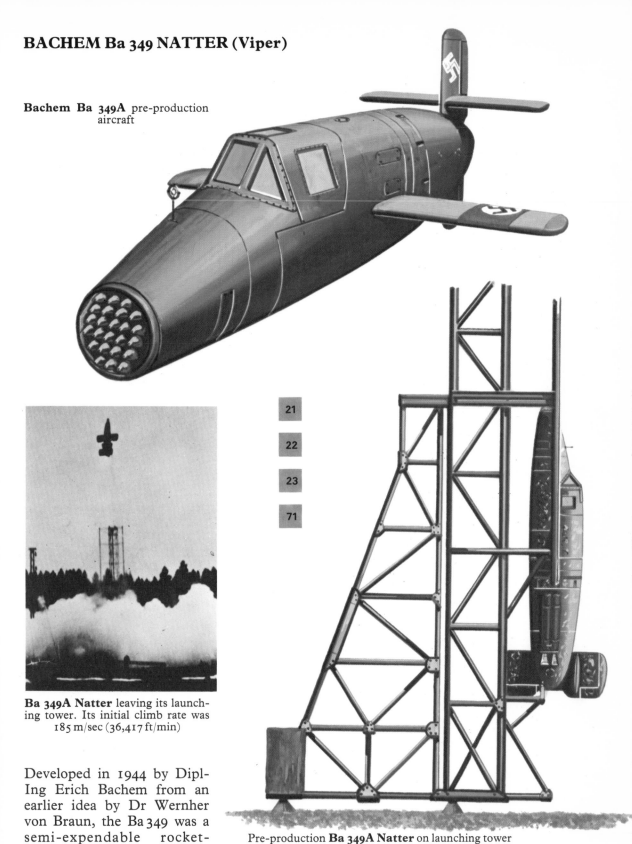

Bachem Ba 349A pre-production aircraft

Ba 349A Natter leaving its launching tower. Its initial climb rate was 185 m/sec (36,417 ft/min)

21
22
23
71

Developed in 1944 by Dipl-Ing Erich Bachem from an earlier idea by Dr Wernher von Braun, the Ba 349 was a semi-expendable rocket-

Pre-production **Ba 349A Natter** on launching tower

powered bomber interceptor designed for launch from a near-vertical ramp. Of 50 ordered, 36 were completed (33 Ba 349As and three Ba 349Bs), and of these 25 had been test-flown by the end of World War 2. None was used operationally. The forward fuselage section contained a well-armoured cockpit and a nose battery of 24 Henschel Hs 217 Föhn (Storm) 73 mm rocket projectiles; after firing these, the pilot released the expendable forward section, himself being ejected to descend by parachute; at the same time, another parachute deployed to bring the recoverable rear section, containing the main rocket motor, safely down to earth. Launch was

Aircraft type			Ba 349A
Power plant			1 × 2,000 kg (4,409 lb) st HWK 509A-1
Accommodation			1
Wing span	m	: ft in	4·00 : 13 1·5
Length overall	m	: ft in	6·25 : 20 6·1
Height overall	m	: ft in	2·25 : 7 4·6
Wing area	m²	: sq ft	4·70 : 50·59
Weight empty	kg	: lb	880 : 1,940
Weight at launch	kg	: lb	2,175 : 4,795
Max speed	km/h	: mph	870 : 540
at (height)	m	: ft	S/L
S/L rate of climb	m/min	: ft/min	10,920 : 35,825
Service ceiling	m	: ft	14,000 : 45,930
Endurance at 797 km/h (495 mph) at 3,000 m (9,845 ft)			2·23 min

aided by four 500 kg (1,102 lb) st Schmidding solid-fuel rockets, jettisoned after launch. These proved unreliable in unpiloted tests, and the first piloted test, on 28 February 1945, resulted in the death of the pilot. About half a dozen successful manned flights were, however, made within the next few weeks.

BLOHM und VOSS BV 40

The BV 40, first flown in late May 1944, was an unpowered bomber interceptor, one of many unorthodox designs by Dr-Ing Richard Vogt. Designed to combat the menace of Allied bombing, it was to be towed into the air behind a standard Bf 109 or Fw 190 fighter, then released to make a frontal or diving attack using the two 30 mm MK 108 cannon mounted beneath the wing roots. A two-wheeled trolley was jettisoned after take-off, landing being made on an extendable under-nose skid and small tail-skid. The pilot lay prone in a heavily-armoured cockpit. Of 19 prototypes ordered, only seven were completed and two others partially completed. These were to have been followed, from March 1945, by 200 production BV 40As, but despite successful testing the BV 40 programme was terminated in autumn 1944. *Data : page 146.*

Two views of the **BV 40 V1 (PN + UA)** single-seat glider fighter, with armoured cockpit for a prone pilot

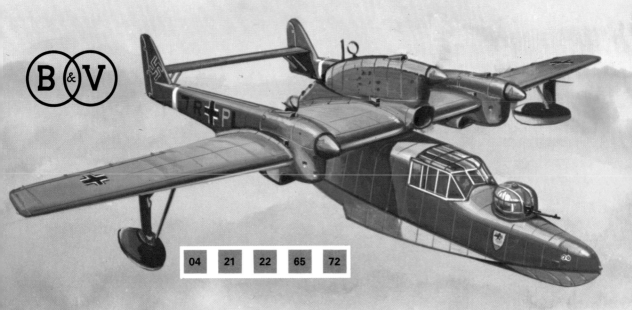

04 | 21 | 22 | 65 | 72

Blohm und Voss BV 138C-1 (7R + PL) of 3.(F)/SAGr 125, based at Constanza, Romania, spring 1943

Staffel emblem of **3.(F)/SAGr 125**

Blohm und Voss BV 138A maritime patrol flying-boat

Staffel emblem of **2./Kü Fl Gr 306**

Aircraft type		BV 138C-1
Power plant		3 × 880 hp Jumo 205D
Accommodation		3
Wing span	m : ft in	26·93 : 88 4·2
Length overall	m : ft in	19·85 : 65 1·5
Height overall	m : ft in	5·90 : 19 4·3
Wing area	m² : sq ft	112·00 : 1,205·56
Weight empty	kg : lb	11,770 : 25,948
Weight loaded (normal)	kg : lb	14,500 : 31,967
Max wing loading	kg/m² : lb/sq ft	129·46 : 26·52
Max power loading	kg/hp : lb/hp	5·49 : 12·11
Max level speed	km/h : mph	285 : 177
at (height)	m : ft	S/L
Cruising speed	km/h : mph	235 : 146
at (height)	m : ft	1,000 : 3,280
Time to 3,170 m (10,400 ft)		24·0 min
Service ceiling	m : ft	5,000 : 16,405
Range (normal)	km : miles	*1,220 : 758

* at 196 km/(122 mph)

BLOHM und VOSS BV 138

This long-serving maritime patrol flying-boat, first flown on 15 July 1937, was a product of Hamburger Flugzeugbau, the aircraft division of the Blohm und Voss shipbuilding concern, and its first two prototypes (D-ARAK and D-AMOR) were designated Ha 138 V1 and V2; both were powered by 600 hp Jumo 205 engines. Higher-powered Jumo 205 C-4s were adopted for the six BV 138 A-0s which followed in 1939 (the 'Ha' designations having been discarded in 1938) and which introduced a redesigned hull shape. The first A-0 flew in February 1939; four were later converted to BV 138 B-0s. Production began in late 1939 of 25 BV 138 A-1s, and two of these were the first to see wartime action, serving as supply transports during the invasion of Norway in April 1940. Main deliveries began two months later to Kü Fl Gr 506 and 906. Following the BV 138 B-0s came, from December 1940, the BV 138 B-1, of which 21 were built. This substituted a 20 mm MG 151 turret-mounted nose cannon for the MG 204 of the A-1, had Jumo 205 D engines, and in its BV 138 B-1/U1 version could carry three 50 kg bombs under the starboard wing centre-section. Other armament comprised a 13 mm MG 131 in an open position above the central engine nacelle, a second MG 151

in a turret at the rear of the hull, and provision for a 7·9 mm MG 15 firing through a starboard hatch. The major version (227 built) was the similar BV 138 C-1, which continued in production until September 1943. A stable and extremely battleworthy aircraft, the BV 138 remained in Luftwaffe service throughout World War 2, serving with some 20 maritime reconnaissance Staffeln from the Atlantic to the Black Sea and from the Arctic to the Mediterranean. A limited number of BV 138 MS (Minensuche: Mine Search) were converted for Minensuchgruppe 1, by fitting 'disarmed' BV 138 C-1s with a large metal hoop for de-gaussing magnetic mines.

BV 138 B-1 with elongated rear hull

BLOHM und VOSS Ha 139 and BV 142

Designed in 1935, the Ha 139 trans-Atlantic mailplane for Deutsche Luft Hansa first flew in late autumn 1936. Three were built: two Ha 139As (V1 and V2) and one slightly larger Ha 139B (V3). All three were operated by DLH until the summer of 1939. By that time four prototypes of the BV 142 had been completed (first flight 11 October 1938), this being essentially a radial-engined landplane counterpart of the Ha 139 V3. All seven were taken over by the Luftwaffe upon the outbreak of war, and five were converted to military standard with an extended, glazed nose and defensive armament. The latter comprised one 7·9 mm MG 15 gun in the nose, one in a dorsal position (turret-mounted in the BV 142 V2/U1) and two in beam positions; the BV 142 V2/U1, in addition, had a fifth MG 15 in a ventral gondola and could carry a 400 kg (882 lb) internal bomb load. All took part in the Norwegian or Danish campaigns in spring 1940, two as reconnaissance aircraft with Kü Fl Gr 406 and 2./Aufkl Gr ob d L, two as supply transports with KGzbV 108; and the BV 142 V3 and V4 as troop transports with KGrzbV 105. The Ha 139 V3 was converted in 1942 to Ha 139B/MS mine counter-measures configuration. *Data: page 146.*

30

Blohm und Voss Ha 139B/MS floatplane, converted from the pre-war DLH mailplane **D-ASTA Nordstern** for mine countermeasures duties, but probably not operational in this role

BV 142 V2/U1 landplane **(PC + BC)**, converted from a pre-war mail transport for maritime reconnaissance and operated by **2./Aufklärungsgruppe ob d L** during 1940–42

BLOHM und VOSS BV 141

One of the most unorthodox aircraft ever to have been built, the BV 141 (originally Ha 141) was designed by Dr-Ing Vogt in 1937 as a private-venture successor to the Henschel Hs 126. The first prototype (D-ORJE) flew on 25 February 1938 with an

Blohm und Voss BV 141B-02 (V10) (NC + RA), as used at **Aufklärungsschule 1**, Grossenhain, autumn 1941

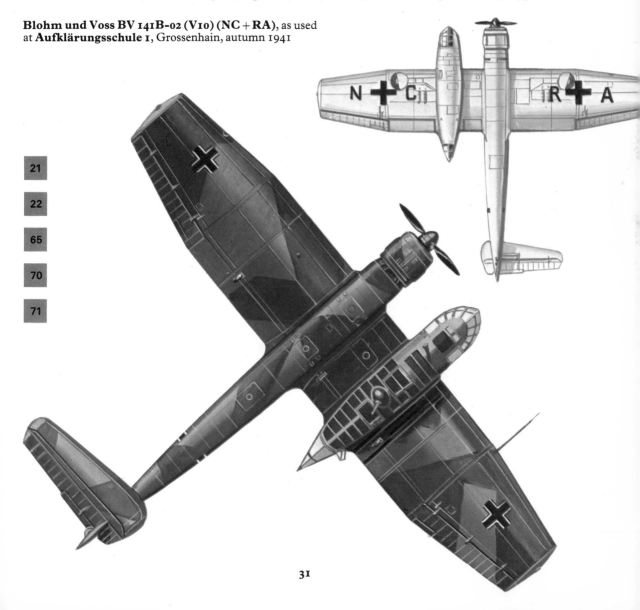

21

22

65

70

71

865 hp BMW 132N engine, a conventional 'stepped' crew nacelle and symmetrical tail-plane. An extensively-glazed nacelle, very similar to that of the contemporary Focke-Wulf Fw 189, appeared on the short-lived second aircraft to fly, and was retained with minor variations on the V3 and the 10 pre-production aircraft which followed. The V3 and the five BV 141A-0s were slightly larger, with two forward-firing MG 17 and two aft-firing nacelle-mounted MG 15 machine-guns (all 7·9 mm calibre) and provision for four 50 kg underwing bombs. The A series, though slightly under-powered, handled well despite their unusual configuration; but repeated troubles of various kinds plagued the five BV 141B-0s, the first of which

Aircraft type			BV 141B-02 (V10)
Power plant			1 × 1,560 hp BMW 801A-0
Accommodation			3
Wing span	m	: ft in	17·46 : 57 3·4
Length overall	m	: ft in	13·95 : 45 9·2
Height overall	m	: ft in	3·60 : 11 9·7
Wing area	m²	: sq ft	52·90 : 569·41
Weight empty	kg	: lb	4,700 : 10,362
Weight loaded (normal)	kg	: lb	5,800 : 12,787
Wing loading	kg/m²	: lb/sq ft	109·64 : 22·46
Power loading	kg/hp	: lb/hp	3·72 : 8·20
Max level speed	km/h	: mph	438 : 272
at (height)	m	: ft	5,000 : 16,405
Cruising speed	km/h	: mph	416 : 258
at (height)	m	: ft	5,650 : 18,535
Service ceiling	m	: ft	10,400 : 34,120
Range (max)	km	: miles	1,900 : 1,180

flew on 9 January 1941. These had more powerful BMW 801 engines, two 20 mm MG FF cannon replacing the MG 17s, and an asymmetrical tailplane. Contrary to reports circulated at the time, no BV 141 was ever operational, though the B-02 (V10) was evaluated in autumn 1941 by Aufklärungsschule 1.

BLOHM und VOSS BV 144

The BV 144 was noteworthy mainly for a design feature popularly regarded as a post-war innovation: it had tilting wings, actuated electro-mechanically to increase the angle of incidence by as much as 9 degrees. Other up-to-date features included slotted flaps, drooping ailerons (linked with the flaps), thermal de-icing of the wing and tailplane leading-edges, and a retractable tricycle landing gear. Accommodation, for 18–23 passengers, included a toilet and fore and aft freight holds. Two prototypes were ordered in 1942 by DLH, which at that time was attempting to plan its post-war commercial fleet and wanted a successor to the venerable Ju 52/3m. Construction was assigned to the captured Breguet factory in France, and the pivoting mechanism was tested on the Ha 140 V3; but by the time the BV 144 V1 was completed in August 1944 Germany was withdrawing from France. After limited further development (but no flight testing) by the French, the BV 144 programme was abandoned. *Data: page 146.*

Blohm und Voss BV 144 short/medium range transport

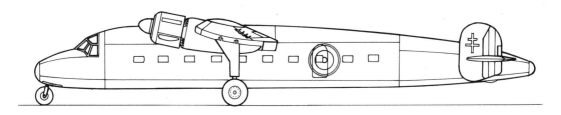

Two views of the **Blohm und Voss BV 155 V3** high altitude fighter under development when the war ended. Note the large wing-mounted radiator fairings

BLOHM und VOSS BV 155

This aircraft had a rather mixed history. The RLM type number 155 was assigned originally to Messerschmitt in early 1942 for a carrier-borne fighter based on, and using components of, the Bf 109. When the German Navy's aircraft carrier programme was halted, Messerschmitt redesigned the aircraft as the Me 155A in late 1942 as a high-speed strike aircraft for the Luftwaffe. With priorities again changing, it was submitted a third time in the spring of 1943 as the Me 155B pressurised, high-altitude interceptor. In August 1943 the RLM reassigned the programme to Blohm und Voss who, not without considerable acrimony, secured permission to redesign it yet again. The first of three Blohm und Voss prototypes flew on 1 September 1944, powered by a turbo-charged DB 603A engine and differing from the Messerschmitt design chiefly in having an entirely new laminar flow wing and a new rear fuselage with enlarged tail surfaces. The BV 155 V2 (first flight 8 February 1945) modified yet again the fuselage, tail, and wing radiators, and introduced an all-round-view cockpit canopy. The V3, captured when only 75% complete, was the prototype for the BV 155C (30 ordered, but none built), which would have had a DB 603U engine, shorter-span wings and fuselage-mounted radiators. Intended armament was two wing-mounted MG 151/20 cannon, and a 30 mm MK 108 firing through the spinner. *Data : page 146.*

BLOHM und VOSS BV 222 WIKING (Viking)

Developed originally to a 1937 DLH order, the prototype BV 222 V1 (D-ANTE) did not fly until 7 September 1940 and was instead used by the Luftwaffe, from July 1941, as an unarmed freight transport. During the following winter it received an armament of two 13 mm MG 131 machine-guns (in two dorsal turrets) and five 7·9 mm MG 81s (one in the nose, two on each side), becoming operational with LTS See 222 in spring 1942. The BV 222 V2, with a deeper hull, joined it in the following August. A new armament standard, to which the V2, V4 and V5 were eventually modified, was set by the V3 (first flight 28 November 1941); this comprised three 20 mm MG 151 cannon (in the forward dorsal and two wing-mounted turrets), one MG 131 (forward beam) and two MG 81s (aft beam). These four Wikings (the V1, V6 and V8 having been lost by then) operated under Fliegerführer Atlantik on maritime reconnaissance from the spring of 1943. These seven prototypes were collectively designated BV 222As. The BV 222B, with Jumo 208 engines, remained unbuilt; the V7, prototype for the BV 222C series, retained the three MG 151s, supplemented by one nose and four beam MG 131s. The V7 and four production

Blohm und Voss BV 222 V1 (X4 + AH) as in service with **Lufttransportstaffel (See) 222**, Tobruk, spring/summer 1942

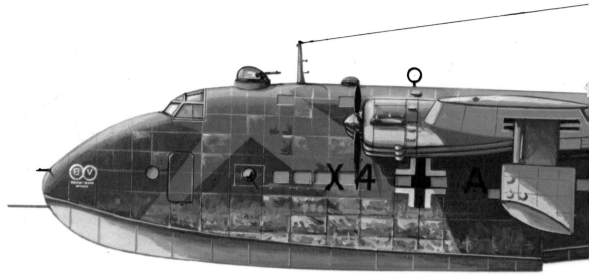

Aircraft type			BV 222A-0 (V4)		
Power plant			6 × 1,200 hp BMW-Bramo 323R-2		
Accommodation			6 + 16		
Wing span	m	: ft in	46·00	: 150	11·0
Length overall	m	: ft in	36·50	: 119	9·0
Height overall	m	: ft in	10·90	: 35	9·1
Wing area	m²	: sq ft	255·00	: 2,744·79	
Weight empty equipped	kg	: lb	28,550	: 62,942	
Weight loaded (max)	kg	: lb	45,600	: 100,531	
Max wing loading	kg/m²	: lb/sq ft	178·82	: 36·63	
Max power loading	kg/hp	: lb/hp	6·33	: 13·96	
Max level speed	km/h	: mph	296	: 184	
at (height)	m	: ft	S/L		
Cruising speed (econ)	km/h	: mph	250	: 155	
at (height)	m	: ft	S/L		
Time to 6,000 m (19,685 ft)			49·0 min		
Service ceiling	m	: ft	6,500	: 21,325	
Range (max)	km	: miles	*7,450	: 4,630	

Above and opposite: The **BV 238 V1 (RO + EZ)**, the largest flying-boat completed by any of the combatant nations during World War 2. It flew for the first time in April 1944, but was destroyed soon afterwards by Allied air attack

Opposite, below: The **BV 222 V1** first prototype during a test flight in the autumn of 1940

* at 4,900 m (16,075 ft)

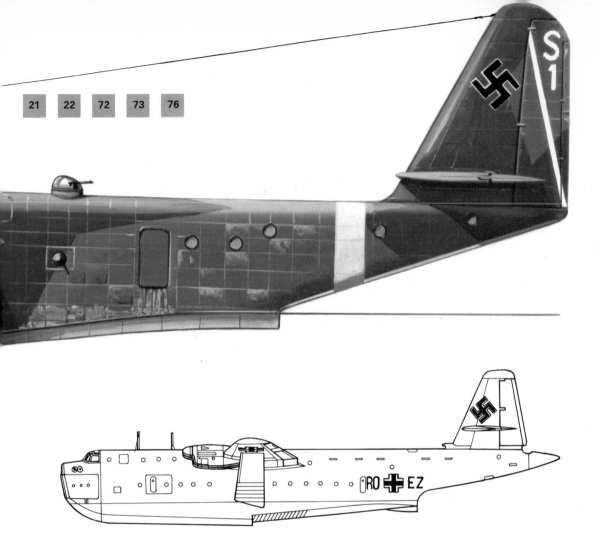

21 22 72 73 76

BV 222C-os entered service in mid-1943 with Aufklärungsstaffel See 222. One other Wiking was completed: the BV 222C-013,

intended as the first Jumo 205D-engined BV 222D but actually fitted, like the rest of the C series, with Jumo 205Cs. Four other C-os remained uncompleted when the programme was halted in 1944.

BLOHM und VOSS BV 238

Although the BV 222 was the largest flying-boat in production during World War 2, Blohm und Voss also completed a single prototype of the even larger BV 238, which first flew in April 1944. Intended to replace the much smaller BV 138, it was originally projected in early 1941 with four Jumo 223 engines, but was later revised for a power-plant of six DB 603s. Of four ordered in the autumn of 1941, the similarly-powered but uncompleted V2 and V3 were likewise to have been prototypes for a production BV 238A, while the V4, with BMW 801 radial engines, was to have foreshadowed a BV 238B series. Blohm und Voss also received a contract for four prototypes of a land-based variant, but the first of these also was incomplete when the war ended. Take-off of the BV 238 V1 was assisted by four 1,500 kg (3,307 lb) st booster rockets. Definitive armament proposed for the BV 238A

comprised no fewer than 22 guns: two 20 mm MG 151 cannon in the dorsal turret; four turrets each with four 13 mm MG 131s in the nose, tail and two wing trailing-edge fairings; and two pairs of MG 131s in beam positions. Twenty 250 kg bombs could be carried within the wings; there was external provision for four 1,200 kg torpedos or 1,000 kg bombs, two BV 143 glider-bombs, or four Hs 293A guided missiles. *Data: page 146.*

Bücker Bü 181 Bestmann two-seat trainer

BÜCKER Bü 181 BESTMANN

This side-by-side two-seat cabin monoplane, developed from the civil Bü 180 Student, was employed by the Luftwaffe primarily as an ab initio and advanced

trainer. First flown in February 1939, the Bü 181 V1 (D-ERBV) was followed by the Bü 181A, deliveries of which began in the latter part of 1940. In addition to various Flugzeugführerschulen, the Bestmann served also with units performing communications and glider-towing duties, and to a lesser extent as a transport for bazooka-type infantry weapons. Production by Bücker amounted to several thousand; in addition, 708 Bü 181As and slightly modified Bü 181Ds were built by Fokker in Holland; 125 were built in Sweden; and 180 in various versions were built by Zlin in Czechoslovakia both during and after the war. A single-seat stablemate, the Bü 182 Kornett (Cornet), flew in 1938, but did not receive any military orders. *Data: page 146.*

DFS 230

In service with LLG 1, 42 DFS 230 assault gliders took part, on 10 May 1940, in the storming of Eben-Emael and three nearby bridges in Belgium, the first time that glider-borne troops had been used in a military operation. Designed by Hans Jacobs of the Deutschen Forschungsinstitut für Segelflug, it first flew in late 1937 and an experimental airborne unit was formed in autumn 1938 with a small pre-production quantity of DFS 230A-os.

Aircraft type			DFS 230A-1
Accommodation			1 + 9/2 + 8
Wing span	m	: ft in	21·98 : 72 1·3
Length overall	m	: ft in	11·24 : 36 10·5
Height overall	m	: ft in	2·74 : 8 11·9
Wing area	m²	: sq ft	41·26 : 444·12
Weight empty	kg	: lb	860 : 1,896
Weight loaded	kg	: lb	2,100 : 4,630
Max wing loading	kg/m²	: lb/sq ft	50·90 : 10·43
Max gliding speed	km/h	: mph	280 : 180
Max aero-tow speed	km/h	: mph	210 : 130
Normal aero-tow speed	km/h	: mph	180 : 112
Best glide ratio (loaded)			18

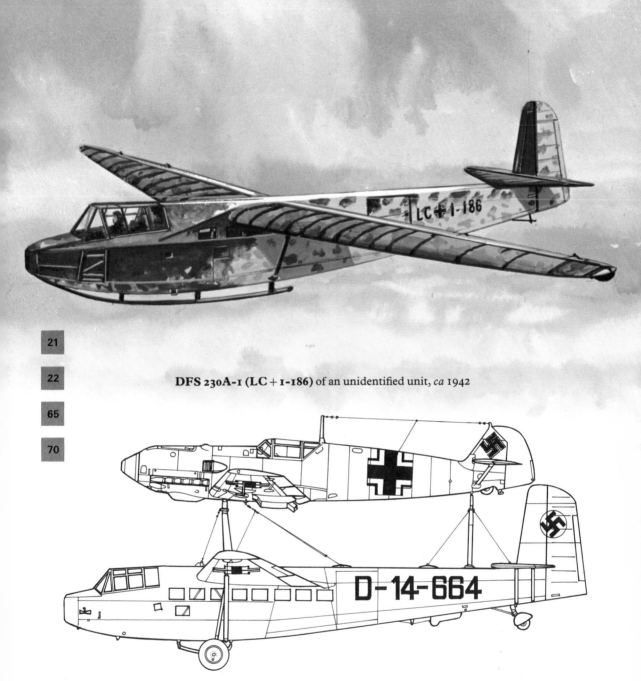

DFS 230A-1 (LC + 1-186) of an unidentified unit, *ca* 1942

Mistelschlepp combination, tested in 1943, of a **Messerschmitt Bf 109E-1** attached to a modified **DFS 230B (D-14-664)**. Although successful, this method of launching the DFS glider was not adopted operationally

Deliveries of the major production DFS 230A-1 and dual-control A-2 began in October 1939, followed about a year later by the improved B-1 and B-2 models. Total DFS 230A/B production amounted to 1,593, from three main German manufacturers (Gotha, Erla and Hartwig) except for 410 built in Czechoslovakia. The B series had a strengthened airframe, an under-fuselage brake 'chute, and a 7·9 mm MG 15 machine-gun aft of the cockpit. Much routine use was made of the DFS 230 as a freighter by various Lastenseglerstaffeln, but from 1941 they figured in airborne operations on the Corinth canal, the invasion of Crete, and the relief of Kholm on the

Eastern Front (1942), Budapest (1945) and Breslau (1945). In September 1943 the spectacular rescue of Mussolini from prison on the Gran Sasso Massif was made possible by a special force of about a dozen DFS 230C-1s, converted from B-1s by adding three Rheinmetall-Borsig braking rockets under the nose. In another attempt to improve the glider's already excellent ability at pin-point landings, a DFS 230B fuselage was fitted with wheels and a three-blade rotor to become the Focke-Achgelis Fa 225 experimental rotor-glider.

DFS 331

Encouraged by the success in 1940 of airborne assault operations involving the DFS 230, the RLM invited the DFS and the Gothaer Waggonfabrik to submit designs for larger-capacity gliders for the same purpose. Hans Jacobs of the DFS designed the DFS 331, of which the sole prototype, the V1, was built by Gotha and test-flown in

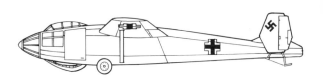

DFS 331 medium transport glider prototype

1941. Features of the DFS 331 included a square-section fuselage of aerofoil profile, to assist lift; a large port-side forward loading door, with an offset 'bubble' canopy above; an extensively-glazed nose, in which a 7·9 mm MG 15 machine-gun was to have been mounted; and twin fins and rudders. Best glide ratio, at fully loaded weight, was 17·5. The RLM, however, selected the competing Go 242 for production. *Data: page 146.*

DORNIER Do 17, Do 215 and Do 217

Three prototypes of the Do 17, each with a single fin and rudder, were built originally as six-passenger high-speed mailplanes for DLH, the Do 17 V1 making its first flight in autumn 1934. DLH turned it down; but the RLM, in search of a new medium bomber, ordered additional prototypes, the first of these (the Do 17 V4) having twin fins and rudders and a shorter fuselage. The V4, V6 and V7 were powered, like the V1 to V3, with two 660 hp Vee-type BMW VI, while the V5 had 775 hp Hispano-Suiza 12 Ybrs engines. The specially-stripped V8, with 1,000 hp boosted DB 600A engines, outclassed even the best single-seat fighters when it appeared at the Zürich International Military Aircraft Competition in July 1937, but by this time the Do 17E-1 bomber and F-1 reconnaissance models, based on the V9, were already in production and service. Both had 750 hp BMW VI 7·3 engines, and the former a

short-range internal bomb load of 750 kg (1,653 lb). While these early versions took part in the Spanish Civil War, the Yugoslav government, also impressed by the V8's performance at Zürich, ordered 20 export Do 17Ks with 980 hp Gnome-Rhône 14 N radial engines, improved speed and range, and a 1,000 kg (2,205 lb) internal weapon load. Luftwaffe production meanwhile continued with the Do 17M bomber (900 hp Bramo 323A-1 supercharged radials), based on the V8, and Do 17P reconnaissance-bomber (865 hp BMW 132Ns), which entered production from late 1937 as successors to the E and F. The experimental Do 17L, R and S appeared in 1937–38, and by September 1938 combined production of the Do 17E, F, M and P for the Luftwaffe had reached 580. After a few Do 17Us, a pathfinder version with DB 600A engines, came the Do 17Z, the most numerous model, of which about 525 were built with Bramo 323A-1 or 1,000 hp Bramo 323P engines.

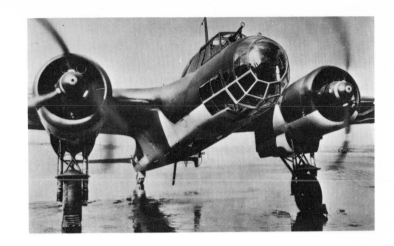

The **Do 17L** was evolved as a four-seat pathfinder version of the Do 17M, but did not go into production; only two prototypes were completed

Production of the Do 17 (about 1,200 of all models) ended in mid-1940. On 2 December 1939 the Luftwaffe had 493 Do 17s on strength; 352 of these were Do 17Zs, most of them probably Z-2 bombers. A small number of Z-3s were converted to Z-10 interim night fighters in 1940. Additional Do 17Ks had been built in 1939–40 by the Yugoslav state aircraft factory, and when Germany invaded that country in April 1941 there were 70 Do 17Ks in service with the Yugoslav Air Force. The few that survived the early fighting were allocated to the Croatian Air Force in early 1942.

Two of the pre-production Do 17Z-0s, redesignated Do 215 V1 and V2, were turned into export demonstrators, powered respectively by Bramo and Gnome-Rhône 14N engines. Only Sweden ordered the Do 215 (18 Do 215A-1s, with DB 601A engines), but these were commandeered before delivery by the Luftwaffe, which went on to order 101 Do 215Bs in several small series. Most of these were similar to one another except the B-5, a night fighter/intruder version with a six-gun 'solid' nose.

By this time, however, mainstream development of the Do 17 was well advanced in the form of the Do 217. The first of many Do 217 prototypes flew in August 1938, outwardly resembling a slightly scaled-up Do 215B. Then came service trials with small batches of Do 217A-0s and C-0s preceding, in 1940, the first major series, the Do 217E. Numerous E sub-types appeared, powered by various models of the BMW 801 radial engine and differing primarily in armament and other equipment. The Do 217E-2, typically, carried up to 2,500 kg (5,512 lb) of bombs internally and a further

The 'splinter' camouflage pattern is well illustrated in this view of the **Do 215 V2**

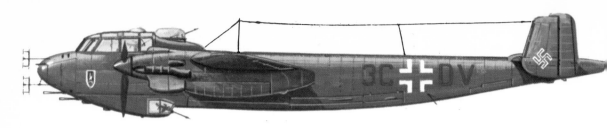

Dornier Do 217N-1 (3C + DV) of 11./NJG 4, France, 1943

1,500 kg (3,307 lb) externally. It was armed with one 15 mm MG 151 cannon and one 7·9 mm MG 15 machine-gun in the nose; one MG 15 on each side at the rear of the cabin; and two 13 mm MG 131 machine-guns—one in a dorsal turret and one in the rear of the under-nose gondola. The Do 217E-5 was a carrier for two underwing Hs 293A radio-controlled glider-bombs. In 1941–42, by which time virtually all Do 17/Do 215 units had re-equipped with Do 217s, the Luftwaffe began converting a number of Do 217 bombers for the night fighter role, the basic modification being to replace the bulbous, glazed nose with a more stream-lined 'solid' one accommodating a battery of guns and, later, radar antennae. First subjects were 157 Do 217E-2s converted into Do 217J-1 intruders and J-2 night fighters, the latter with Lichtenstein BC radar. Both had four 20 mm MG FF cannon and four 7·9 mm MG 17 machine-guns in the nose,

Dornier Do 17Z-2 (U5 + DL) of 3./KG 2 'Holzhammer', Balkans theatre, spring 1941

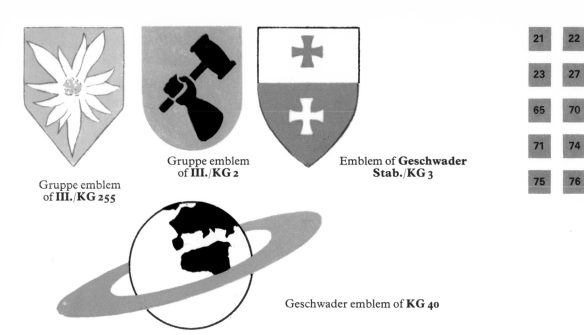

Gruppe emblem
of **III./KG 255**

Gruppe emblem
of **III./KG 2**

Emblem of **Geschwader
Stab./KG 3**

21	22
23	27
65	70
71	74
75	76

Geschwader emblem of **KG 40**

Dornier Do 217K-1 (Z6 + BH) of I./KG 66, Chartres, summer 1943

A **Dornier Do 17Z-2 (U5 + AH) of Kampfgeschwader 2.** The Do 17Z was widely used during the campaigns in Poland, France and the Low Countries, and in the Battle of Britain

A **Do 215B-4 (PK + EM)** in factory markings. This reconnaissance version carried two aerial cameras, one of them in the 'chin' blister fairing

Dornier Do 217E-4/R19 **(U5 + NT)** in the markings of **KG 2 'Holzhammer'**. This model had BMW 801C engines and balloon cable-cutters on the wing leading-edges

An apparently hybrid **Do 217J** night fighter. Normally the J-1 had no Lichtenstein BC nose radar array, and the J-2 had no rear bomb bay, but this aircraft clearly has both

plus provision for one 13 mm MG 131 ventral gun and another in the dorsal turret. The next bomber series, the Do 217K (1,700 hp BMW 801D engines), featured a further-redesigned and even more bulbous nose than the E series. The K-2 and K-3 could carry anti-shipping weapons beneath extended-span (24·80 m; 81 ft 4·4 in) wings. Vee-type engines—1,750 hp DB 603As—appeared on the Do 217M bomber series, otherwise similar to the K-1; and on the Do 217N-1 and N-2 night fighters which, in 1943, began replacing the J series. The final model was the Do 217P pressurised reconnaissance version, of which, however, only six development aircraft were built. Total Do 217 output, ending in June 1944, amounted to 1,905, of which all except 364 were bombers. The five Do 217Rs were in fact Do 317A-0 missile carriers, redesignated.

Aircraft type			Do 17Z-2	Do 217K-1	****Do 217N-1
Power plant			2 × 1,000 hp BMW-Bramo 323P	2 × 1,700 hp BMW 801D	2 × 1,750 hp DB 603A
Accommodation			4	4	4
Wing span	m	: ft in	18·00 : 59 0·7	19·00 : 62 4·0	19·00 : 62 4·0
Length overall	m	: ft in	15·79 : 51 9·7	16·98 : 55 8·5	18·90 : 62 0·1
Height overall	m	: ft in	4·55 : 14 11·1	4·97 : 16 3·7	5·00 : 16 4·9
Wing area	m²	: sq ft	55·00 : 592·01	57·00 : 613·54	57·00 : 613·54
Weight empty equipped	kg	: lb	5,210 : 11,486	8,900 : 19,621	10,280 : 22,663
Weight loaded	kg	: lb	8,590 : 18,937	16,580 : 36,553	13,200 : 29,101
Max wing loading	kg/m²	: lb/sq ft	156·18 : 31·98	290·88 : 59·57	231·57 : 47·40
Max power loading	kg/hp	: lb/hp	4·29 : 9·46	4·88 : 10·75	3·77 : 8·31
Max level speed	km/h	: mph	360 : 224	515 : 320	515 : 320
at (height)	m	: ft	4,000 : 13,125	4,000 : 13,125	6,000 : 19,685
Cruising speed	km/h	: mph	300 : 186	400 : 248	425 : 264
at (height)	m	: ft	4,000 : 13,125	4,000 : 13,125	5,400 : 17,715
Time to 1,000 m (3,280 ft)			3·3 min	3·5 min	3·0 min
Service ceiling	m	: ft	7,000 : 22,965	8,200 : 26,905	8,900 : 29,200
Range	km	: miles	*1,160 : 720	**2,300 : 1,429	***1,755 : 1,090

* with 500 kg (1,102 lb) bomb load and aux fuel   ** with max internal fuel   *** normal   **** weights and performance for N-2; N-1 similar

DORNIER Do 18

Evolved to fulfil joint civil and military requirements for a successor to the Dornier Wal, the Do 18a or V1 first prototype (D-AHIS) first flew on 15 March 1935. A total of about 160 was eventually built during 1936–40, of which the major versions were the Do 18D (approx 75 built) and Do 18G and H (71 built) for the Luftwaffe. The Do 18D-1, D-2 and D-3, differing in equipment only, were delivered from mid-1936 and by autumn 1939 equipped single Staffeln of five Küstenfliegergruppen. Powered by 600 hp Jumo 205C engines, they were lightly armed with single (bow and dorsal) 7·9 mm MG 15 machine-guns and could carry two 50 kg bombs beneath the starboard wing. The Do 18G-1 entered service from mid-1939, having uprated Jumo 205Ds, a 13 mm MG 131 in the bow and a 20 mm MG 151 in a dorsal turret, and provision for rocket-assisted take-off. The Do 18H-1 was a six-seat unarmed trainer version. Do 18Ds figured in many early campaigns, among them Poland, Norway and the Battle of Britain. They and the later G model had been withdrawn from first-line service by autumn 1941, but a number of G-1s were then converted to Do 18N-1s for air/sea rescue duties with various Seenotstaffeln.

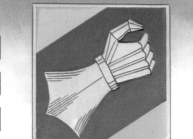

DORNIER Do 24

Of the 294 Do 24s built (including proto-types), only 37 saw service with the Nether-lands East Indies Navy, for whom it was originally designed in 1935; by contrast, some 220 were employed by the Luftwaffe.

04	21
22	65
72	73

A **Dornier Do 18D of Küstenfliegergruppe 406**, which operated this type until the late summer of 1941

First example to fly, on 3 July 1937, was the Do 24 V3 (D-AYWI), powered by 875 hp Wright Cyclone R-1820-F52 radial engines; this aircraft, the V4, and 10 similarly-powered Do 24K-1s were delivered to the Dutch Navy, and apart from the Jumo 205C-engined V1 and V2 were the only German-built examples of the flying-boat. Production continued with 28 Dutch-built K-2s (1,000 hp R-1820-G102 engines, revised armament) for the NEI, of which 25 were delivered. The other three, plus eight partially-built K-2s, were captured in 1940 and completed to Luftwaffe standards as Do 24N-1 air/sea rescue aircraft, with a further change in armament. From this were developed the major ASR/transport version, the Do 24T-1, of which 180 were built (110

Dornier Do 24T-1 (CH + EW) of the Seenotdienstführer Mittelmeer (Sea Rescue Service Mediterranean), Syracuse, 1943

Staffel emblem of
3./Seenotgruppe

Aircraft type		Do 18G-1	Do 24T-1
Power plant		2 × 880 hp Jumo 205D	3 × 1,000 hp BMW-Bramo 323R-2
Accommodation		4	6
Wing span	m : ft in	23·70 : 77 9·1	27·00 : 88 7·0
Length overall	m : ft in	19·25 : 63 1·9	22·05 : 72 4·1
Height overall	m : ft in	5·45 : 17 10·6	5·75 : 18 10·4
Wing area	m² : sq ft	98·00 : 1,054·86	108·00 : 1,162·50
Weight empty	kg : lb	5,980 : 13,184	9,400 : 20,723
Weight loaded (max)	kg : lb	10,795 : 23,799	16,200 : 35,715
Max wing loading	kg/m² : lb/sq ft	110·15 : 22·56	150·00 : 30·72
Max power loading	kg/hp : lb/hp	6·13 : 13·52	5·40 : 11·90
Max level speed	km/h : mph	267 : 166	332 : 206
at (height)	m : ft	1,000 : 3,280	2,600 : 8,530
Cruising speed (max)	km/h : mph	228 : 142	295 : 183
at (height)	m : ft	1,000 : 3,280	2,600 : 8,530
Time to 2,000 m (6,560 ft)		17·5 min	6·0 min
Service ceiling	m : ft	4,200 : 13,780	5,300 : 17,390
Range (normal)	km : miles	3,500 : 2,175	2,900 : 1,802

Dornier Do 24N-1 (CM + EH) of the Seenotdienstführer Mittelmeer, 1942

Dornier Do 24T-1 air/sea rescue and transport flying-boat

in Holland, 70 by SNCAN in France); 49 Dutch-built Do 24T-2s with minor equipment changes; and 12 generally similar Dutch-built Do 24T-3s for Spain. Only 48 of the French-built T-1s reached the Luftwaffe, the remainder being 'liberated' and serving with Flottille 9F Tr of the French Aéronavale. The NEI Dorniers operated for some time against Japanese shipping in the south-west Pacific; those of the Luftwaffe saw action in the Baltic, English Channel, Mediterranean, Black Sea and other areas with KGzbV 108 See and with various Seenotstaffeln and Seetransportstaffeln.

DORNIER Do 26

Of clean and advanced layout, the Do 26 was designed in 1937 as a trans-Atlantic mail carrier for DLH, which ordered three with three more on option. Only these six were completed, the V1 (D-AGNT) flying for the first time on 21 May 1938. The V1 and V2 (Do 26A) were operated on South Atlantic mail services prior to World War 2; the V3, with a cabin for four passengers, and the V4 to V6 (eight passengers) were then, with the V1 and V2, taken over by the Luftwaffe and converted to Do 26D standard as reconnaissance and transport aircraft, armed with a 20 mm MG 151 cannon in a bow turret, two 7·9 mm MG 15 machine-guns in waist positions and a third MG 15 in the rear floor of the hull. Allocated initially to Kü Fl Gr 406 (later 506), two were destroyed by RAF Hurricanes during the Denmark/Norway campaigns, and the remainder were eventually withdrawn to communications duties. *Data : page 146.*

The sixth and last **Do 26, the V6 (P5 + DH)**, in the markings of **Sonderstaffel Tranz-Ozean**

DORNIER Do 317

One of four contenders for an He 111/Ju 88 replacement, the Do 317 was designed originally in 1939 as a pressurised, twin-engined medium bomber with a 3,600 km (2,237 mile) range, 600 km/h (373 mph) top speed, 2,000 kg (4,409 lb) internal bomb load, and remote-controlled armament. Development took third place to the Fw 191 and Ju 288, but was revived in 1941 as a Do 217 replacement. However, of six Do 317A prototypes ordered, only the V1 was completed, flying in 1943. This unarmed prototype could carry 3,000 kg (6,614 lb) of bombs internally, but high-altitude performance was disappointing and the proposed longer-span Do 317B was abandoned later that year. The remaining five Do 317As on order were in fact completed as unpressurised Do 217Rs. They were issued to III./KG 100 in autumn 1944, but saw little or no operational service. *Data : page 146.*

The **V1** sole prototype (**VK + IY**) of the **Dornier Do 317**

DORNIER Do 335 PFEIL (Arrow)

Reviving a principle patented in 1937, Dornier designed the radical centreline-thrust Do 335 to a 1942 requirement for a day/night fighter, fighter-bomber and reconnaissance aircraft. The Do 335 V1 (CP + UA) first flew at Oberpfaffenhofen on 26 October 1943, with one 1,800 hp DB 603E engine in the nose and another, driving a pusher propeller, in the rear fuselage. By the war's end, 36 Do 335s had been completed: 13 Versuchs (prototype) aircraft, 10 pre-production A-0s, 11 A-1s, and two A-12 tandem two-seat trainers; over 80 other A-series aircraft remained uncompleted. First armed prototype was the V5; the V9 was prototype for the A series, which had two 15 mm MG 151/15 guns in the upper forward fuselage and a 30 mm MK 103 cannon firing through the front spinner. The A-1 could carry one 500 kg or two 250 kg bombs internally. No Do 335s saw combat service, though operational evaluation of the Do 335A-0 was carried out from autumn 1944 by Erprobungskommando 335. Prototypes for other versions included the Do 335A-4 (one A-0 converted for unarmed photo-reconnaissance; the V10 (A-6) tandem two-seat night fighter; the V11 (A-10) and V12 (A-12) tandem-seat trainers; and the V13 (B-1) and V14 (B-2) Zerstörern. Uncompleted prototypes included the V4 (Do 435) night fighter, with side-by-side seats and 2,500 hp Jumo 222 engines; and the V15 to V20, prototypes for the B-1, B-2 and B-3 Zerstörern and the B-6 and B-7 night fighters. The B-4 and B-8 were proposed high altitude versions, with extended span, the corresponding trainer version being the B-5. The Do 635 (later redesignated Ju 8-635) was a long range reconnaissance project (see illustration overleaf).

Dornier Do 335 VII, prototype for the Do 335A-10 series, 1944

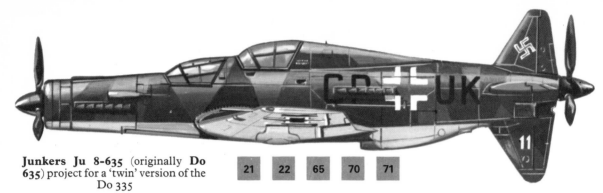

Junkers Ju 8-635 (originally **Do 635**) project for a 'twin' version of the Do 335

| 21 | 22 | 65 | 70 | 71 |

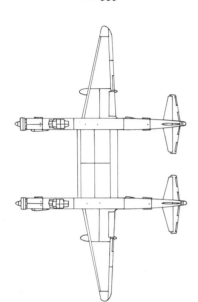

Aircraft type			Do 335A-0
Power plant			2 × 1,750 hp DB 603A-2
Accommodation			1
Wing span	m	: ft in	13·80 : 45 3·3
Length overall	m	: ft in	13·85 : 45 5·3
Height overall	m	: ft in	5·00 : 16 4·8
Wing area	m²	: sq ft	38·50 : 414·41
Weight empty	kg	: lb	6,530 : 14,396
Weight loaded	kg	: lb	9,510 : 20,966
Max wing loading	kg/m²	: lb/sq ft	247·01 : 50·59
Max power loading	kg/hp	: lb/hp	2·72 : 5·99
Max level speed	km/h	: mph	732 : 455
at (height)	m	: ft	7,100 : 23,295
Cruising speed	km/h	: mph	633 : 393
at (height)	m	: ft	5,700 : 18,700
Time to 8,000 m (26,245 ft)			14·5 min
Service ceiling	m	: ft	9,500 : 31,170
Range	km	: miles	2,150 : 1,336

Dornier Do 335A-07, one of several A-os used by **Erprobungskommando 335** in late 1944

FZG 76 (V-1) flying bomb in typical 1944 colour scheme

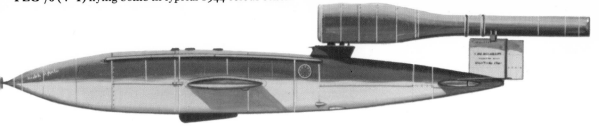

Aircraft type		Fi 103	
Power plant		1 × 300 kg (661 lb) st As 109–014	
Wing span (untapered)	m : ft in	5·30 : 17	4·7
Length overall	m : ft in	7·90 : 25	11·0
Body diameter	m : ft in	0·838 : 2	9·0
Wing area	m² : sq ft	4·80 : 51·67	
Weight empty	kg : lb	815 : 1,796	
Warhead	kg : lb	850 : 1,874	
Weight loaded	kg : lb	2,180 : 4,806	
Max level speed	km/h : mph	645 : 401	
at (height)	m : ft	2,000 : 6,560	
Launching speed	km/h : mph	378 : 235	
Service ceiling	m : ft	3,000 : 9,845	
Range (typical)	km : miles	240 : 149	

FIESELER Fi 103

Known alternatively as the FZG 76 (Flakzielgerät: anti-aircraft aiming device 76) or Vergeltungswaffe Eins (Reprisal Weapon 1), or more simply as the V1, the Fi 103 flying bomb had an airframe designed by Dipl-Ing Robert Lüsser of Fieseler, and a Siemens guidance system.

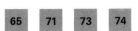

Fieseler Fi 103 **Reichenberg II** two-seat glider trainer

Fieseler Fi 103 **Reichenberg III**

It could be launched from a 50 m (152 ft) inclined ramp by a Walter steam-driven catapult, or air-dropped from a carrier aircraft (usually an He 111). The weapons were launched against Britain (from 13 June 1944) and targets in continental Europe, and more than 30,000 were manufactured by Henschel, Mittelwerke and Volkswagen factories. An Askania gyroscope fed signals to the elevators and rudder to control attitude and direction, and the terminal dive was initiated when a pre-set distance had been flown. Operational air launches were

mostly made from He 111Hs of KG 3 (later KG 53); but, whatever the launch method, about a quarter of the weapons failed in use and only about a quarter of the remainder got through Allied defences. Even more of a desperation weapon was the 'Reichenberg' piloted series, of which there were four versions: the single-seat and two-seat unpowered Fi 103R-I and R-II, the single-seat powered R-III trainer, and the proposed operational R-IV. About 175 were so converted, but none was used in combat.

| 21 | 22 | 23 | 65 | 70 | 71 | 79 | 80 |

Fieseler Fi 156D-1 ambulance aircraft of an unidentified unit, Romania, 1943. **Inset: Fi 156C-2 (CB + VD)** in North Africa, *ca* spring 1941

FIESELER Fi 156 STORCH (Stork)

The Storch Army co-operation, reconnaissance, ambulance and communications light-plane was in Luftwaffe service from early 1938 until the end of the war, attached to almost every major unit in virtually every European, North African, Mediterranean and Russian theatre. Fieseler built about 1,950, Morane-Saulnier 784 and Mraz in Czechoslovakia about 150, and examples

served also with the air forces of Bulgaria, Croatia, Finland, Hungary, Romania, Slovakia, Spain, Sweden, Switzerland, the USSR and Yugoslavia. The first of five prototypes (D-IKVN) was flown in spring 1936, followed in 1937 by the Fi 156A-0 and A-1. The Fi 156C-0 of late 1938, which mounted a defensive 7·9 mm MG 15 gun in the rear of the cabin, was followed by C-1 (unarmed liaison/staff transport) and C-2 (reconnaissance) models, and the 270 hp

Aircraft type		Fi 156C-1	
Power plant		1 × 240 hp As 10C-3	
Accommodation		*2–3	
Wing span	m : ft in	14·25 : 46	9·0
Length overall	m : ft in	9·90 : 32	5·8
Height overall	m : ft in	3·05 : 10	0·0
Wing area	m² : sq ft	26·00 : 279·86	
Weight empty equipped	kg : lb	978 : 2,156	
Weight loaded	kg : lb	1,260 : 2,778	
Wing loading	kg/m² : lb/sq ft	48·46 : 9·93	
Power loading	kg/hp : lb/hp	5·25 : 11·57	
Max level speed	km/h : mph	175 : 109	
at (height)	m : ft	S/L	
Cruising speed	km/h : mph	150 : 93	
at (height)	m : ft	S/L	
Time to 1,000 m (3,280 ft)		3·9 min	
Service ceiling	m : ft	5,200 : 17,060	
Range (at 150 km/h; 93 mph)	km : miles	330 : 205	

* Weights and performance for 2-seater

As 10P-engined multi-purpose C-3 and C-5. The C-5 had provision to carry three 50 kg bombs, a 135 kg mine, a camera pod or a drop-tank. Specialised rescue models were the Fi 156D-0 (As 10C) and D-1 (As 10P) of 1940–41, with space for a stretcher in a roomier cabin with easier access. The Storch could take off in 70 m (230 ft) and land in 26 m (85 ft) or less, and many became personal transports of senior officers. The Fi 256 was a five-seat civil development, of which Morane-Saulnier built two prototypes.

FIESELER Fi 167

Proving far superior to the Arado Ar 195 with which it originally competed, the Fi 167 was intended as a carrier-based dive-bomber/torpedo-bomber/reconnaissance aircraft. The first of two prototypes, designed by Reinhold Mewes, flew in mid-1938; these were followed by 12 pre-production Fi 167A-0s (first flight early 1940), armed with a forward-firing 7·9 mm MG 17 gun in the front fuselage, to starboard, and a movable 7·9 mm MG 15 in the rear cockpit. A 765 kg torpedo, up to 1,000 kg of bombs, or a drop-tank, could be carried externally. Germany's fluctuating interest in aircraft carriers led to the Fi 167 programme being abandoned, but nine of the A-0s underwent coastal trials in Holland with the specially-formed Erprobungsstaffel 167 from 1940–43, after which some of them were sold to Romania. *Data : page 146.*

The pre-production **Fieseler Fi 167A-05 (TJ + AN)**

Flettner Fl 282 helicopter taking off from Morane-Saulnier's airfield at Puteaux, France, *ca* 1943–44. In the foreground is **DP + NC**, one of the two **Fieseler Fi 256** prototypes

FLETTNER Fl282 KOLIBRI (Hummingbird)

Developed from the Fl265, of which six were built for the German Navy, the Fl282 fleet spotter helicopter first flew in 1941 after 30 prototypes and 15 pre-production examples had been ordered in the previous year. In 1944 the RLM ordered 1,000 of these helicopters from BMW, but Allied air attacks prevented production from beginning and by the

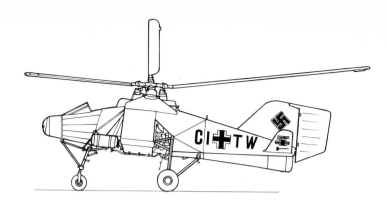

Flettner Fl 282B-1 Kolibri (CI + TW) two-seat observation helicopter

war's end only 24 prototypes had been built and only three of these survived. Several were used operationally from 1942 onwards, usually flown from platforms above the gun turrets of convoy escort vessels in Baltic, Aegean and Mediterranean waters; they exhibited excellent control and performance qualities, despite often severe weather conditions. Projects under development in 1945 were the Fl285 fleet spotter, powered by an Argus As 10C engine and able to carry two small bombs, and the Fl339 transport helicopter, powered by a BMW 132A engine. *Data : page 146.*

FOCKE-ACHGELIS Fa 223 DRACHE (Dragon)

The Fa 266 Hornisse (Hornet) five/six-seat civil transport helicopter, evolved for Deutsche Lufthansa from the technology used in Prof Henrich Focke's practical helicopter, the Fw 61, was adapted after the outbreak of World War 2 as a potential multi-purpose military helicopter, the Fa 223, of which the V1 prototype first flew on 3 August 1940. This aircraft (D-OCEB) had a four-seat compartment in the extensively-glazed forward part of the fuselage, the powerplant being installed aft of this cabin and driving two counter-rotating rotors mounted on outriggers. Official Luftwaffe acceptance trials in early 1942 resulted in orders for 30 pre-production and 100 production Fa 223Es, but Allied bombing prevented all except a second prototype, 17 of the pre-production and nine production Drachen from being completed during the war, most of them with Bramo 323Q-3 engines. Eventual production was planned at up to 400 per month in 1944, but the few Fa 223s built saw only limited operational service, either for rescue or as transports with LTS 40. Unfinished projects included a crane helicopter, the Fa 284, able to lift a 7,000 kg (15,432 lb) slung load on the power of two 2,000 hp BMW engines; and one for two Fa 223s united in tandem by a new fuselage centre-section. *Data : page 146.*

Focke-Achgelis Fa 223 Drache transport helicopter (DM + SR)

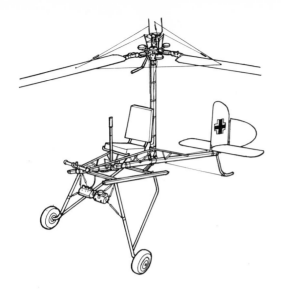

FOCKE-ACHGELIS Fa 330
BACHSTELZE (Water Wagtail)

Evolved as a more realistic alternative to the Arado Ar 231, the Fa 330 was a foldable single-seat rotor-kite, which could extend considerably the viewing radius of a surfaced U-boat by being towed on a 150 m (492 ft) cable above and behind the submarine. About 200 were built, by Weser Flugzeugbau, and they served from mid-1942 principally in the Indian Ocean and Gulf of Aden. Later models had a larger rotor of 8·53 m (28 ft). *Data : page 147*.

FOCKE-WULF Fw 44
STIEGLITZ (Goldfinch)

Dipl-Ing Kurt Tank's first design for Focke-Wulf, and the company's first major international success, the Fw 44 was in widespread use before the war, both as a civil sporting biplane and as a standard basic aircrew trainer for the embryo Luftwaffe. It was designed in 1931 and first flew in the late summer of 1932, a small series of Fw 44Bs with 120 hp Argus As 8 in-line engines soon giving way to the major production model, the radial-engined Fw 44C. German manufacture, by several companies, amounted to several hundred, many of which were exported to Bolivia, Chile, China, Finland, Romania and Turkey. Foreign licences were acquired by Argentina (for 500 Fw 44Js by FMA), Austria (40 by Hirtenberg), Brazil (for 40 Fw 44Js by Fábrica do Galeão), Bulgaria (as the state aircraft factory's DAR-9), Czechoslovakia (for 600 by SKD) and Sweden (for 85 by ASJA and the RSwAF Workshop). Many Fw 44Cs remained in Luftwaffe service during World War 2, with the Flugzeugführerschulen and one or two Luftkriegsschulen. *Data : page 147*.

Formation of **Fw 44C** tandem two-seat training biplanes, photographed at Bromberg in August 1940

Focke-Wulf Fw 44C fitted for winter operations with skis on all three points of the landing gear

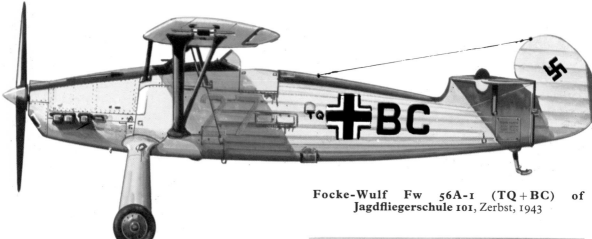

Focke-Wulf Fw 56A-1 (TQ + BC) of **Jagdfliegerschule 101,** Zerbst, 1943

FOCKE-WULF Fw 56 STÖSSER (Falcon)

This aerobatic parasol monoplane was designed by Dipl-Ing Kurt Tank in 1932 as a home defence fighter, and the Fw 56a or V1 (D-ISOT) first flew in November 1933. The V2, with bomb racks and an elementary release gear, was evaluated as a dive-bombing trainer, but the Stösser was eventually employed by the Luftwaffe, to whom Fw 56A-1 deliveries began in 1936, as a fighter trainer and advanced trainer. Armed with one or two 7·9 mm MG 17 machine-guns, it could also carry three 10 kg bombs. Production (close on 1,000, including three prototypes and three A-os) continued until 1940, recipients including the NSFK and

Focke-Wulf Fw 56A Stösser advanced trainer

the air forces of Austria (12) and Hungary (18). Luftwaffe Fw 56A-1s were a major type at the JFS and FFS throughout the war; at least one (CA + GN of JFS 112) was used in pick-a-back experiments with a DFS 230 glider.

FOCKE-WULF Fw 57

Although abandoned in late 1936, the Fw 57 was an original contender for the RLM's 1934 Kampfzerstörer ('heavy' fighter-bomber) requirement. In the event, this was revised into separate specifications resulting in the Bf 110 and Ju 88, but the overweight, underpowered Fw 57, with its poor flying qualities, would in any case have been unlikely to succeed. Intended armament comprised two 20 mm MG FF cannon in the nose, a third 20 mm gun in a power-operated dorsal turret, and an internal load of six 100 kg bombs. Three prototypes were flown,

Focke-Wulf Fw 57 V2 (second prototype) three-seat 'heavy' fighter-bomber

the V1 for the first time in the late spring of 1936. *Data : page 147.*

FOCKE-WULF Fw 58 WEIHE (Kite)

Kurt Tank's Fw 58, preferred to Arado's Ar 77 design, became the Luftwaffe's approximate equivalent of Britain's Airspeed Oxford: an aircrew trainer, ambulance and general-purpose hack transport. Several hundred were built by four German factories, and others were licence-built in Brazil and Hungary. There were 13 prototypes, of which the V1 first flew in spring 1935; the V2, V4 and V11 were, respectively, the basic development aircraft for Fw 58A, B and C

production series. Only a small number of Fw 58As were built, the Fw 58B being essentially an improved A with a glazed nose mounting for one 7.9 mm MG 15 machine-gun. A second MG 15 was ring-mounted aft of the crew cabin, and the Fw 58B could also carry twelve 10 kg bombs, some being used in an anti-partisan role in Bulgaria in 1944. The solid-nosed Fw 58C, the main wartime production variant, was a six-passenger transport with 260 hp Hirth HM 508D engines.

Aircraft type		Fw 56A-1	Fw 58B
Power plant		1 × 240 hp As 10C-3	2 × 240 hp As 10C-3
Accommodation		1	4
Wing span	m : ft in	10·55 : 34 7·4	21·00 : 68 10·8
Length overall	m : ft in	7·62 : 25 0·0	14·00 : 45 11·2
Height overall	m : ft in	2·55 : 8 4·4	4·20 : 13 9·4
Wing area	m² : sq ft	14·00 : 150·69	47·00 : 505·90
Weight empty	kg : lb	670 : 1,477	1,870 : 4,123
Weight loaded	kg : lb	985 : 2,171	2,900 : 6,393
Max wing loading	kg/m² : lb/sq ft	70·36 : 14·41	61·70 : 12·64
Max power loading	kg/hp : lb/hp	4·10 : 9·05	6·04 : 13·32
Max level speed	km/h : mph	268 : 166	255 : 158
at (height)	m : ft	S/L	S/L
Cruising speed	km/h : mph	245 : 152	238 : 148
at (height)	m : ft	S/L	S/L
S/L rate of climb	m/min : ft/min	510 : 1,673	330 : 1,083
Service ceiling	m : ft	6,200 : 20,340	5,400 : 17,715
Range	km : miles	370 : 230	600 : 373

04

21

22

23

65

70

Focke-Wulf Fw 190A-4/Trop. (unit unknown), North Africa, 1943

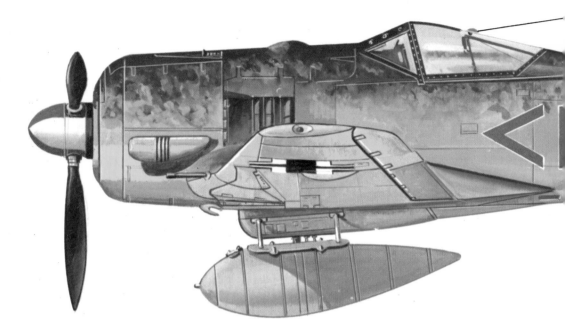

FOCKE-WULF Fw 190 and Ta 152

The Fw 190 V1 (D-OPZE), designed by Dipl-Ing Kurt Tank and Oberingenieur R. Blaser to a 1938 RLM requirement, first flew on 1 June 1939, this aircraft and the V2 each being powered by a 1,550 hp BMW 139 two-row radial engine. Subsequent aircraft, with the larger and more powerful BMW 801C, included 40 pre-series Fw 190A-0s ordered in 1940, most of them with a 1·00 m (3 ft 3·4 in) greater wing span which later became standard. Full-scale production started with 100 four-gun Fw 190A-1s, which entered service with II./JG 26 in summer

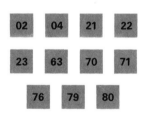

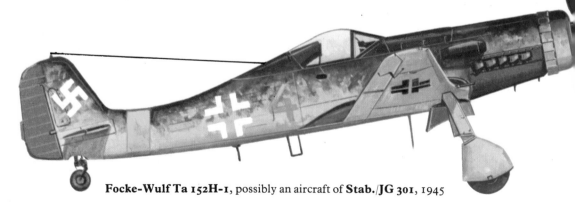

Focke-Wulf Ta 152H-1, possibly an aircraft of **Stab./JG 301**, 1945

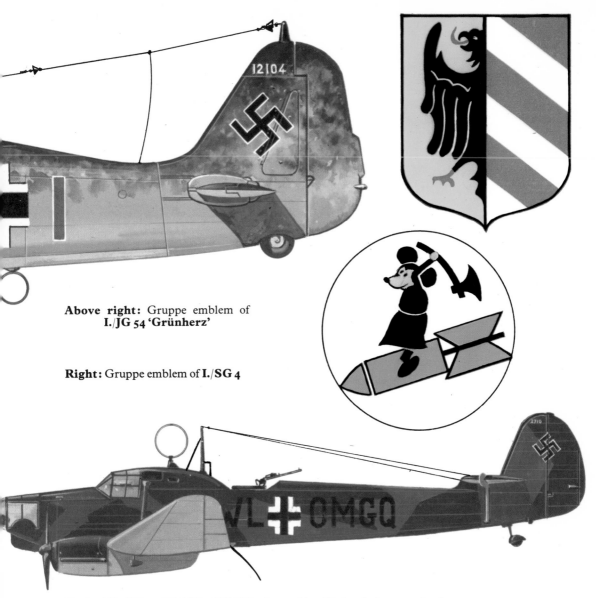

Above right: Gruppe emblem of **I./JG 54 'Grünherz'**

Right: Gruppe emblem of **I./SG 4**

Focke-Wulf Fw 58B (WL-OMGQ) of an unidentified unit, late 1939/early 1940

1941, and continued with the better-armed A-2 and A-3, the latter having six guns (two MG 151/20 and four MG 17) and a BMW 801D-2 engine. Early operational use was made of the Fw 190 in the Jagdbomber role, in low-level hit-and-run raids over southern England during 1942. The A-4 series (2,100 hp boosted BMW 801D-2) included the A-4/U8 fighter-bomber (carrying a drop-tank and 500kg; 1,102 lb of bombs, with armament reduced) and the A-4/R6 bomber interceptor with underwing rocket projectiles. By the end of 1942 more than 2,000 Fw 190s had been delivered and were in widespread service in Europe, the Mediterranean and on the Eastern Front. The A-5 was produced chiefly for close support; the A-6 and A-7 featured further improvements in firepower; the A-8s were mostly bomber interceptors or Zerstörern,

Focke-Wulf Fw 190A-4/R6 equipped with underwing launching tubes for two W Gr 21 rocket missiles, a weapon used with some success in the bomber interception role

Fw 190F-8 with MG 131 machine-guns in a bulged cowling, under-fuselage rack for a 250 kg bomb, and underwing racks for four 50 kg bombs

Fw 190 V53 (DU + UC), converted from an A-7 as a pre-production (D-0) development aircraft for the long-nosed Fw 190D series with Jumo 213A-1 engine

Focke-Wulf Fw 190 V30/U1 (GH + KT), converted from an Fw 190C as the second development aircraft for the high altitude Ta 152H fighter

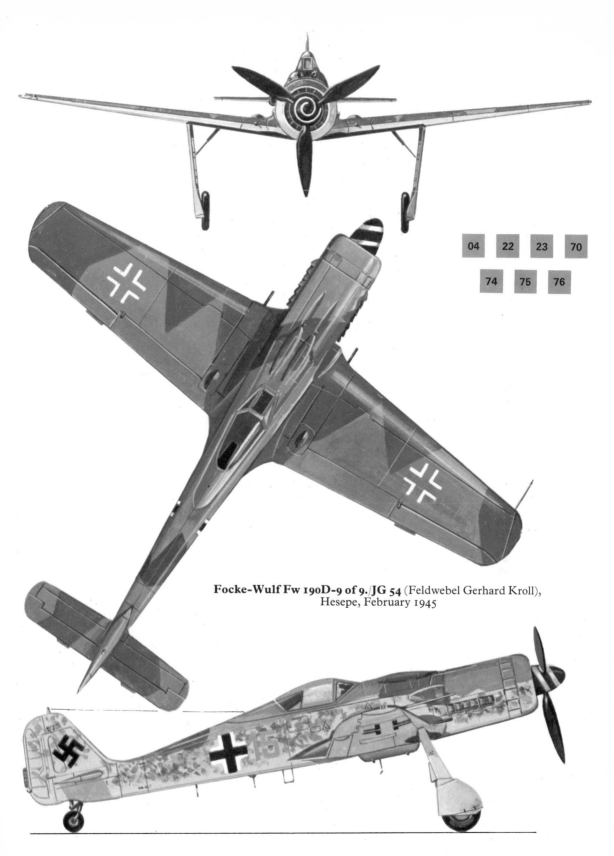

04 22 23 70

74 75 76

Focke-Wulf Fw 190D-9 of 9./JG 54 (Feldwebel Gerhard Kroll),
Hesepe, February 1945

Aircraft type		Fw 190A-8	Fw 190D-9	Ta 152H-1
Power plant		1 × 1,700 hp BMW 801 D-2	1 × 1,776 hp Jumo 213A-1	1 × 1,750 hp Jumo 213E-1
Accommodation		1	1	1
Wing span	m : ft in	10·506 : 34 5·6	10·506 : 34 5·6	14·44 : 47 4·5
Length overall	m : ft in	8·95 : 29 4·4	10·192 : 33 5·3	10·71 : 35 1·6
Height overall	m : ft in	3·96 : 12 11·9	3·36 : 11 0·3	3·36 : 11 0·3
Wing area	m² : sq ft	18·30 : 196·98	18·30 : 196·98	23·30 : 250·80
Weight empty equipped	kg : lb	3,470 : 7,650	3,490 : 7,694	3,920 : 8,642
Weight loaded	kg : lb	4,380 : 9,656	4,840 : 10,670	4,750 : 10,472
Max wing loading	kg/m² : lb/sq ft	239·34 : 49·02	264·48 : 54·17	203·86 : 41·75
Max power loading	kg/hp : lb/hp	2·57 : 5·68	2·72 : 6·01	2·71 : 5·98
Max level speed	km/h : mph	657 : 408	686 : 426	760 : 472
at (height)	m : ft	6,300 : 20,670	6,600 : 21,655	12,500 : 41,010
S/L rate of climb	m/min : ft/min	716 : 2,349	950 : 3,117	1,050 : 3,445
Service ceiling	m : ft	10,300 : 33,790	11,300 : 37,075	14,800 : 48,555
Range (internal fuel)	km : miles	800 : 497	837 : 520	1,215 : 755

although some were employed as all-weather fighters and others as two-seat trainers. The Fw 190B and C series were discarded, after a few prototypes with boosted BMW 801D or DB 603A engines, in favour of the long-nosed Fw 190D or 'Dora'. The D series, of which some 650–700 were built, evolved from prototypes with the 1,776 hp Jumo 213A-1 engine, fitted with an annular cooling duct that maintained the 'radial' appearance. Early Fw 190D-0s and D-1s were characterised, apart from their longer cowlings, by lengthened rear fuselages and (on the D-1) increased fin area. The major production version (numbered to follow on from the A-8) was the Fw 190D-9 interceptor, which entered service with III./ JG 54 in 1944 and was armed with two MG 151/20 wing cannon and two MG 131s over the engine. Regarded by many as the Luftwaffe's finest piston-engined fighter of the war, the Fw 190D-9 was to have been followed by the D-11, 12, 13, 14 and 15; but no substantial production of these models was undertaken. The Fw 190F and G (the E reconnaissance fighter and high altitude H series not being built) were short-nosed models, based on the Fw 190A. The Fw 190F series' principal model, the F-8, had provision for underwing rocket projectiles. Both the F and G were BMW 801-powered, the latter being mostly fighter-bombers in which gun armament was reduced to permit (on the G-1) a single 1,800 kg (3,968 lb) bomb, or (on other G models) up to 1,000 kg (2,205 lb) of smaller bombs, to be carried. Total Fw 190 production, which ended in 1945, was approximately 19,500. It was the first fighter to give the Luftwaffe a combat advantage over the early Spitfires. Its overall versatility, too complex to list here, was characterised by several dozen kits to adapt production aircraft to different roles, and the allocation of some 80 Versuchs numbers to individual development aircraft.

Several of the latter helped in evolving the Ta 152, virtually a total redesign, derived from the Fw 190D and first flown in autumn 1944. First production (and only operational) series was the Ta 152H, with long-span wings for high altitude flying, which saw limited service with JG 301 in 1945. Proposed variants included the Ta 152A, B, E and S; but the only other version to begin serious development before the war ended was the Ta 152C (2,100 hp DB 603L), first flown in November 1944.

FOCKE-WULF Ta 154

This wooden-construction night and bad-weather fighter was unofficially dubbed 'Moskito', but there the similarity to its British namesake ended. One of Germany's least successful wartime ventures, it was designed in little more than nine months, the Ta 154 V1 (TE + FE) flying for the first time on 1 July 1943 with two 1,350 hp Jumo 211R

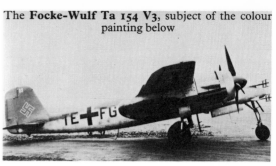

The **Focke-Wulf Ta 154 V3**, subject of the colour painting below

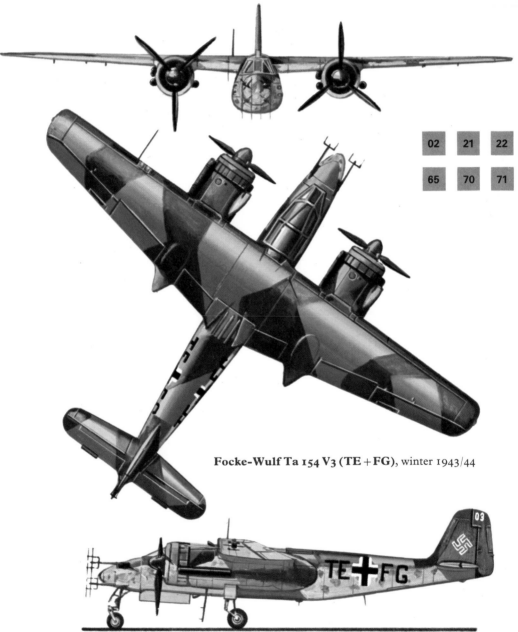

02	21	22
65	70	71

Focke-Wulf Ta 154 V3 (TE + FG), winter 1943/44

engines. Flight tests produced a top speed of 700 km/h (435 mph), but revealed also a need to strengthen the forward fuselage to absorb the stress from firing the two 30 mm MK 108 and two 20 mm MG 151 cannon with which the Ta 154 was to be armed. The Ta 154A-03/U1 (or V3), first flown on 25 November 1943, carried full armament and Lichtenstein C-1 radar, and was powered by 1,750 hp Jumo 213Es. Fifteen Versuchs/pre-production aircraft were completed, and production of several hundred was planned, but the entire programme was halted in August 1944 and only 10 Ta 154A-1s were built. At least two of these were lost in crashes, resulting from structural failures due to weaknesses in the bonding materials used, but the remainder were employed briefly on operations during the winter of 1944/45 by I./NJG 3 and NJGr 10. The A-0s were later converted and evaluated as the lower components of Mistel composite aircraft, carrying an Fw 190 director fighter on their backs, or as other types of expendable bomber destroyer; but

Aircraft type			Ta 154A-1
Power plant			2 × 1,750 hp Jumo 213E
Accommodation			2
Wing span	m	: ft in	16·00 : 52 5·9
Length overall	m	: ft in	12·57 : 41 2·9
Height overall	m	: ft in	3·60 : 11 9·7
Wing area	m²	: sq ft	32·40 : 348·75
Weight empty	kg	: lb	6,405 : 14,120
Weight loaded (max)	kg	: lb	9,550 : 21,054
Max wing loading	kg/m²	: lb/sq ft	294·75 : 60·37
Max power loading	kg/hp	: lb/hp	2·73 : 6·02
Max level speed	km/h	: mph	650 : 404
at (height)	m	: ft	7,100 : 23,295
Time to 8,000 m (26,250 ft)			14·5 min
Service ceiling	m	: ft	10,900 : 35,760
Range (max)	km	: miles	*1,365 : 848

* on internal fuel at 7,000 m (22,965 ft)

none was used operationally in this way. Abandoned with the programme were the proposed Ta 154C-1 (with) and C-2 (without radar), each with 1,776 hp Jumo 213A engines, a longer fuselage carrying more fuel, and two extra MK 108 cannon in a dorsal Schräge Musik installation; and the proposed Ta 254A (Jumo 213) and Ta 254B (DB 603), developed from the Ta 154C with a 30 per cent larger wing.

FOCKE-WULF Fw 187

The Fw 187 was designed in 1935 as a single-seat twin-engined fighter. Two prototypes were built to this configuration, the V1 (D-AANA, first flown in late spring 1937) having 680 hp Jumo 210Da engines and the V2 670 hp Jumo 210Gs. There followed the V3, V4 and V5, adapted to the two-seat Zerstörer role, with Jumo 210Gs (in shorter nacelles), a lengthened canopy, and provision for two 7·9 mm MG 17 and two 20 mm MG FF guns flanking the nose; and the V6, the only example to be fitted with the 1,000 hp DB 600A engines for which the original fighter had been designed. Preferring the Messerschmitt Bf 110, the RLM

sanctioned only three Jumo-engined pre-production Fw 187A-0s, these having two additional forward-firing MG 17s. They were used on local defence of Focke-Wulf's Bremen factory in mid-1940; briefly (and unofficially) on operations by 13.(Z)/JG 77 in Norway in the 1940/41 winter; and one at least by the LSS at Vaerlose, Denmark, in 1942. Hindsight says that the Fw 187 should have been the Luftwaffe's Zerstörer. The V6 was 60 km/h (37 mph) faster than the Bf 109E; and even the lower-powered A-0, which handled superbly, was superior to the Bf 110C-1 in wing loading, power/weight ratio and, especially, climbing and turning rates.

Fw 187A-0 bearing bogus 'unit markings' for propaganda purposes

Focke-Wulf Fw 187A-0 (GA+WZ) of the **Luftschiesschule at Vaerløse**, summer 1942

21 22 65 70 71

Aircraft type		Fw 187A-0	
Power plant		2 × 700 hp Jumo 210Ga	
Accommodation		2	
Wing span	m : ft in	15·30 : 50	2·4
Length overall	m : ft in	11·10 : 36	5·0
Height overall	m : ft in	3·85 : 12	7·6
Wing area	m² : sq ft	30·40 : 327·22	
Weight empty	kg : lb	3,700 : 8,157	
Weight loaded	kg : lb	5,000 : 11,023	
Max wing loading	kg/m² : lb/sq ft	164·47 : 33·69	
Max power loading	kg/hp : lb/hp	3·42 : 7·55	
Max level speed	km/h : mph	530 : 329	
at (height)	m : ft	4,200 : 13,780	
Time to 6,000 m (19,685 ft)		5·8 min	
Service ceiling	m : ft	10,000 : 32,810	

FOCKE-WULF Fw 189 UHU (Owl)

The Fw 189 was designed in early 1937 as a short range tactical reconnaissance successor to the Hs 126, competing with the Ar 198 and BV 141. The Fw 189 V1 (D-OPVN), with 430 hp Argus As 410 engines, flew in July 1938. The Fw 189B, based on the V5, was first to enter production (three B-0 and ten B-1). This was a five-seat, unarmed dual-control trainer, and entered service in spring 1940. Major production series (828 built, including ten pre-production A-0s) was the Fw 189A, based on the V4. The A-1, which entered service in autumn 1940, was armed with a 7·9 mm MG 17 gun in each

Focke-Wulf Fw 189A-2 (5D + FH) of 1.(H)/31,
Eastern Front, summer 1942

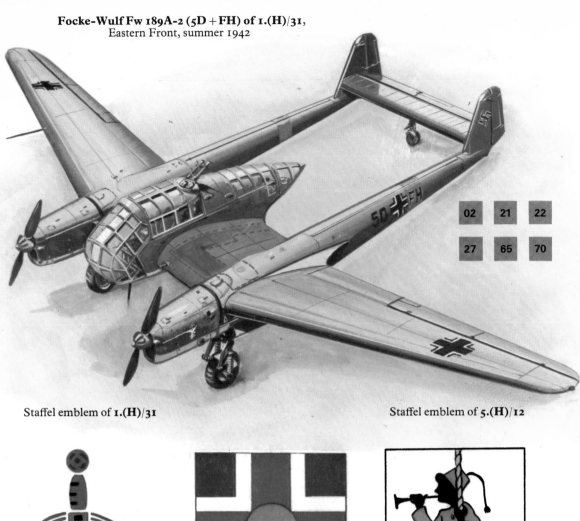

02	21	22
27	65	70

Staffel emblem of **1.(H)/31**

Staffel emblem of **5.(H)/12**

National insignia of the **Slovak Air Force**

wing root and two MG 15s of similar calibre, one in the top and one in the tailcone of the central nacelle. However, these early Fw 189As were only lightly armed, and MG 81Z (twin MG 81) guns replaced each MG 15 in the Fw 189A-2, the MG 17s being replaced in the A-4 by 20 mm MG FF cannon. These models could each carry four 50 kg bombs beneath the wings; the Fw 189A-3 was a two-seat unarmed trainer.

The only other production variant was the Fw 189F-1, similar to the A-2 but with 580 hp As 411MA-1 engines. Total production, including prototypes, was 864: 217 by Focke-Wulf, 337 by Aero in Czechoslovakia (1941–43) and 310, including 17 F-1s, by Sud-Ouest in France (1942–44). Fourteen A-1s were supplied to Slovakia, and about 30 A-2s to Hungary. The Luftwaffe's Fw 189s served with at least nine Aufkl Gr

Aircraft type			Fw 189A-2		
Power plant			2 × 465 hp As 410A-1		
Accommodation			3		
Wing span	m	: ft in	18·40	: 60	4·4
Length overall	m	: ft in	12·03	: 39	5·6
Height overall	m	: ft in	3·10	: 10	2·0
Wing area	m²	: sq ft	38·00	: 409·03	
Weight empty equipped	kg	: lb	3,245	: 7,154	
Weight loaded (normal)	kg	: lb)	3,950	: 8,708	
Max wing loading	kg/m²	: lb/sq ft	109·74	: 22·47	
Max power loading	kg/hp	: lb/hp	4·48	: 9·88	
Max level speed	km/h	: mph	350	: 218	
at (height)	m	: ft	2,400	: 7,875	
Cruising speed (max)	km/h	: mph	325	: 202	
at (height)	m	: ft	2,400	: 7,875	
Time to 4,000 m (13,125 ft)			8·3 min		
Service ceiling	m	: ft	7,300	: 23,950	
Range (normal)	km	: miles	670	: 416	

The yellow bands around the tail-booms of this **Fw 189A** indicate service on the Eastern Front, an area in which this reconnaissance aircraft was used extensively

and fifteen NAGr; some became extempore night fighters with I./NJG 100; and others were employed for communications, casualty evacuation and other second-line duties. Models which did not achieve production included the attack Fw 189C, with a much smaller, heavily armoured two-seat nacelle; the twin-float Fw 189D; and the re-engined Fw 189E (700 hp Gnome-Rhône 14M) and Fw 189G (950 hp As 402).

FOCKE-WULF Fw 191

Six prototypes of the Fw 191 were ordered, but only three were completed. It was designed to a winter 1939/40 specification for a pressurised medium bomber, and the unpressurised V1 and V2 both flew in early 1942, each with two 1,600 hp BMW 801MA engines and dummy armament. Seriously underpowered, they were also grossly overweight with the equipment necessary to operate their all-electric main systems. The V6 (first flight spring 1943) had hydraulic main systems and 2,200 hp Jumo 222 engines (the intended powerplant), but was still unsatisfactory, and the programme was halted later that year, cancelling the proposed Fw 191A, B and C production models. *Data : page 147.*

Focke-Wulf Fw 191 V1 prototype high altitude medium bomber

Focke-Wulf Fw 200C-4 (F8 + CD) of Stab. II./KG 40, autumn 1942

FOCKE-WULF Fw 200 CONDOR

From August 1940 to January 1941, operating over the eastern Atlantic from Norway to Biscay, either alone or partnered by U-boats, Condors sank more than 360,000 tons of Allied merchant shipping. Their success waned only with the advent of such Allied long range aircraft as the Beaufighter, Mosquito and Liberator, CAM-ship Hurricanes, and fighters from the first escort carriers. Designed as a 26-passenger transport for Deutsche Lufthansa (the Fw 200 V1, D-AERE *Saarland*, first flew on 27 July 1937), the Fw 200A and B entered service pre-war with DLH and with Brazilian and Danish airlines. Two prototypes, acquired by the RLM, later served as Luftwaffe VIP transports, but the first maritime patrol/bomber was the Fw 200C, based on the V10. The first operational Condors were a few unarmed Bs and C-os equipping KGrzbV 105 in 1940 as transports during the invasion of Norway, and six armed C-os operating with a reconnaissance Staffel. The Fw 200C-1 had 830 hp BMW 132H engines,

a crew of five, and an armament of two 7·9 mm MG 15 machine-guns in the upper fuselage, with a third MG 15 and a 20 mm MG FF cannon in the offset ventral gondola. This also contained the bomb-aiming position and an attachment for a 250 kg marker bomb; four HE bombs of similar size, or two 1,000 kg mines, could be carried beneath the outboard engines and outer wings. The C-1 entered service in the maritime role in late 1940, with KG 40; it was followed in 1941 by the slightly-modified C-2. The C-3 was strengthened (several early Condors having broken their backs in landing accidents), and had more powerful engines, a sixth crew member (seven in some variants), a variety of armament installations, and a maximum bomb load of 2,095 kg (4,620 lb). Principal sub-type was the C-4, produced from February 1942, with Rostock or Hohentweil search radar and improved radio. Later production models included the C-6 and C-8, able to carry an Hs 293A glider-bomb beneath each outboard nacelle. By the time the C-8 appeared, armament had increased

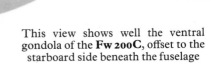

Geschwader
emblem of **KG 40**

This view shows well the ventral gondola of the **Fw 200C**, offset to the starboard side beneath the fuselage

Aircraft type			Fw 200C-3/U4
Power plant			4 × 1,200 hp BMW-Bramo 323R-2
Accommodation			7
Wing span	m	: ft in	32·85 : 107 9·3
Length overall	m	: ft in	23·45 : 76 11·2
Height overall	m	: ft in	6·30 : 20 8·0
Wing area	m²	: sq ft	120·00 : 1,291·67
Weight empty	kg	: lb	12,950 : 28,550
Weight loaded	kg	: lb	22,700 : 50,045
Max wing loading	kg/m²	: lb/sq ft	189·17 : 38·74
Max power loading	kg/hp	: lb/hp	4·73 : 10·43
Max level speed	km/h	: mph	360 : 224
at (height)	m	: ft	4,800 : 15,750
Cruising speed	km/h	: mph	335 : 208
at (height)	m	: ft	4,000 : 13,125
S/L rate of climb	m/min	: ft/min	390 : 1,280
Service ceiling	m	: ft	5,800 : 19,030
Range (standard fuel)	km	: miles	3,560 : 2,212

to a forward dorsal turret (one 20 mm MG 151), rear dorsal turret (one 13 mm MG 131), one nose and two beam positions (each with one MG 131), and a single MG 15 in the rear of the gondola. Including prototypes and civil models, 276 Condors had been built when production ended in early 1944. By that time the Condor had conceded the maritime reconnaissance role to the Ju 290A, leaving itself (and the He 177) to concentrate primarily upon attacking already located targets. Other Fw 200s were transferred to transport duties, notably on the Eastern Front, and, in particular, in support of the beleaguered German army near Stalingrad in early 1943. The DLH Condors, too, continued to operate transport services until the closing weeks of the war.

GOTHA Go 145

The Go 145a first flew in February 1934, and the Go 145A production version entered service with Luftwaffe basic training units from 1935. Subsequent versions included the experimental Go 145B (enclosed cockpits and 'spatted' main undercarriage); Go 145C gunnery trainer (one or two 7·9 mm MG 15 machine-guns); and Go 145D (240 hp As 410 engine). Production totalled almost 10,000, including contributions from AGO, BFW and Focke-Wulf, CASA in Spain (25) and the Turkish state aircraft factory. Thirty were supplied to the Slovakian Air Force. The Go 145 served with numerous FFS and, from 1942–45, as a night 'nuisance' raider behind Soviet lines

Gotha Go 145A (KE + WF) tandem two-seat training biplane

with several Störkampfstaffeln, carrying up to 70 kg (154 lb) of 2 kg or 4 kg bombs. One Go 145 (D-IIWS) flew in the spring of 1941 with a 120 kg (265 lb) st Argus pulse-jet engine—forerunner of the powerplant for the Fi 103 flying bomb—beneath the fuselage. *Data : page 147.*

GOTHA Go 242 and Go 244

A direct result of early wartime success with the DFS 230, the larger Go 242 transport/assault glider was ordered 'off the drawing board' of Dipl-Ing Kalkert in autumn 1940, two prototypes being flown in the following spring. The Go 242A-1 freighter had deeper tailbooms than the pre-production A-0, and was delivered from August 1941; the assault-troop A-2 was similar except for a brake parachute. Go 242As first appeared in Greece, Sicily and North

Africa in early 1942, usually towed by Heinkel He 111s and sometimes having rocket-assisted take-off.

Aircraft type		Go 242A-1	
Accommodation		2 + 21	
Wing span	m : ft in	24·50 : 80	4·6
Length overall	m : ft in	15·80 : 51	10·0
Height overall	m : ft in	4·40 : 14	5·2
Wing area	m² : sq ft	64·40 : 693·20	
Weight empty equipped	kg : lb	3,236 : 7,134	
Weight loaded (max)	kg : lb	7,300 : 16,093	
Max wing loading	kg/m² : lb/sq ft	113·35 : 23·22	
Max gliding speed	km/h : mph	290 : 180	
Max aero-tow speed	km/h : mph	240 : 149	
Ceiling with Ju 52/3m	m : ft	2,200 : 7,220	
Ceiling with He 111 or Bf 110	m : ft	3,800 : 12,465	

04 21 22 75 77 78

Gotha Go 242A-1 (F7 + 8-12) on an unidentified Feldflugplatz on the Eastern Front, 1943

NARVIK

Gotha Go 244B-1 (4V + ES) of
8./TG 3, Hagenow, summer 1942

04	21
22	23
70	78

Aircraft type			Go 244B-1	
Power plant			2 × 700 hp Gnome-Rhône 14M 06/07	
Accommodation			2 + 21	
Wing span	m	: ft in	24·50 : 80	4·6
Length overall	m	: ft in	15·90 : 52	2·0
Height overall	m	: ft in	4·70 : 15	5·0
Wing area	m²	: sq ft	64·40 : 693·20	
Weight empty equipped	kg	: lb	5,224 : 11,517	
Weight loaded (max)	kg	: lb	7,162 : 15,789	
Max wing loading	kg/m²	: lb/sq ft	111·21 : 22·78	
Max power loading	kg/hp	: lb/hp	5·12 : 11·29	
Max level speed	km/h	: mph	290 : 180	
at (height)	m	: ft	4,000 : 13,125	
Cruising speed (max)	km/h	: mph	270 : 168	
at (height)	m	: ft	3,900 : 12,795	
Time to 5,000 m (16,405 ft)			17·0 min	
Service ceiling	m	: ft	8,350 : 27,395	
Range (S/L max)	km	: miles	480 : 298	

The original six Gotha Staffeln formed the basis for the later Schleppgruppen, serving also as supply and evacuation transports on the Eastern Front. A non-jettisonable wheeled landing gear characterised the B series, which comprised the B-1 and B-2; their B-3 and B-4 personnel counterparts with rear exit doors; and the B-5 trainer. A few A-1s were converted to C-1s, a water-landing version delivered to 6./KG 200 in autumn 1944 for an attack (never mounted) on the Home Fleet at Scapa Flow. Of 1,528 Go 242s built, 133 B-1 to B-5s were converted (and another 41 built new) as powered Go 244B-1 to B-5s, most with captured French Gnome-Rhône engines and others with 660 hp BMW 132Zs or captured Soviet 750 hp Shvetsov M-25As. Underpowered and vulnerable, they were withdrawn in 1942 after only a few months' limited service, mostly in the Mediterranean and southern Russia, and allocated to the training of airborne troops.

HEINKEL He 46

The He 46 reconnaissance air-craft had been largely replaced by the Hs 126 before the war, but a few continued in this role for a time with the Luftwaffe and the Hungarian Air Force, armed with an MG 15 gun and small bombs. *Data : page 147.*

HEINKEL He 51

This pre-war, single-seat fighter/close support aircraft had, by World War 2, been withdrawn to fighter training duties with the Jagdflieger-schulen, continuing in this role until 1945. Two MG 17 guns were mounted over the engine. *Data : page 147.*

HEINKEL He 59

Serving in 1939 with various Seenotstaffeln for air/sea rescue and four Kü Fl Gr for coastal reconnaissance, minelaying and anti-shipping duties, the He 59 remained active in these roles during the early war years; it also helped to land troops in Norway and Holland in the spring of 1940. First flown in September 1931, it underwent service trials as the He 59A and He 59B-1, after which

Aircraft type		He 59B-2	He 60C
Power plant		2 × 660 hp BMW VI 6·0 ZU	1 × 660 hp BMW VI 6·0 ZU
Accommodation		4	2
Wing span	m : ft in	23·70 : 77 9·1	12·92 : 42 4·7
Length overall	m : ft in	17·40 : 57 1·0	11·50 : 37 8·8
Height overall	m : ft in	7·10 : 23 3·5	4·94 : 16 2·5
Wing area	m² : sq ft	153·20 : 1,649·03	54·00 : 581·25
Weight empty	kg : lb	5,000 : 11,023	2,410 : 5,313
Weight loaded	kg : lb	9,100 : 20,062	3,556 : 7,840
Max wing loading	kg/m² : lb/sq ft	59·40 : 12·17	65·85 : 13·48
Max power loading	kg/hp : lb/hp	6·89 : 15·20	5·39 : 11·87
Max level speed	km/h : mph	220 : 137	225 : 140
at (height)	m : ft	S/L	1,000 : 3,280
Cruising speed	km/h : mph	185 : 115	190 : 118
at (height)	m : ft	S/L	1,000 : 3,280
Time to 2,000 m (6,560 ft)		4·7 min	8·9 min
Service ceiling	m : ft	3,500 : 11,485	5,000 : 16,405
Range (standard fuel)	km : miles	940 : 584	*770 : 478

* at 2,000 m (6,560 ft)

Heinkel He 60C (D1+AH) of 1./SAGr 126, Aegean theatre, *ca* spring 1942

Gruppe emblem of **SAGr 126**

140 B-2s and B-3s were built by Arado, the former armed with single nose, dorsal and ventral 7·9 mm MG 15 guns. Most were later converted by the Walter Bachmann Flugzeugbau for air/sea rescue (He 59C-2 and D-1) or specialised training in navigation (He 59C-1, D-1 and N), torpedo dropping (E-1) and photographic roles (E-2); all of these aircraft except the He 59N were unarmed.

HEINKEL He 60

This reconnaissance biplane, first flown in early 1933, once equipped all major German warships but was mainly shore-based by 1939. About 200 mainstream He 60Cs and Ds, each with a single rear-cockpit MG 15 gun, were built by Arado and Weser. When

Heinkel He 59C-2 (D-ARYX) of an unidentified **Seenotstaffel,** English Channel/North Sea area, 1940

Geschwader emblem of
KG 4 'General Wever'

Gruppe emblem of
III./KG 53
'Legion Condor'

their intended replacement (the He 114) failed to impress, they were retained by SAGr in the North Sea, Baltic and Eastern Mediterranean areas until 1943, then being gradually redeployed for communications and training duties.

HEINKEL He 111

It was in early 1934 that Walter and Siegfried Günter of the Ernst Heinkel AG began work on the design of this all-metal low-wing twin-engined mono-plane, and the first prototype, the He 111 V1, emerged at the end of that year as a remark-ably clean-looking and efficient aircraft. With two 660 hp BMW VI liquid-cooled in-verted-Vee engines, it flew for the first time on 24 February 1935, fitted out as a medium

Geschwader emblem of
KG 55

Personal emblem painted on
an **He 111H-6 of St G 3**

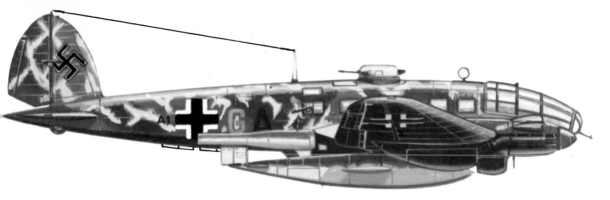

Heinkel He 111H-22 (A1 + GA) of Stab./KG 53 (the Netherlands, *ca* October/November 1944), with Fieseler Fi 103 mounted beneath the starboard wing root

An **He 111** about to take off for a night mission during the Battle of Britain

An **He 111** bomber bearing the diving eagle emblem of **KG 30 'Adler'**

04	21	22	23	24
27	65	70	71	

Heinkel He 111H-16 (5J + GN) of 5./KG 4 in temporary use as a transport, Stalino, winter 1942/43

bomber prototype with provision for a 1,000 kg (2,205 lb) internal load of bombs, stowed upright, and an armament of three 7·9 mm MG 15 machine-guns, in nose and dorsal positions and in a retractable ventral 'dustbin'. Three more prototypes followed, of which the V2 (D-ALIX) and V4 (D-AHAO) were completed as commercial transports accommodating 10 passengers and a cargo of mail. Some efforts were made to interest the state airline, Deutsche Luft Hansa, in the He 111 as a commercial venture, and when the aircraft's existence was made public officially, in January 1936, the German authorities tried to convince all and sundry that the He 111 was purely a civil type, although its true purpose was more than obvious. However, DLH did later operate a handful of He 111Cs and Gs.

The He 111 V3 (D-ALES) served as a prototype for the initial pre-production military version, the He 111A-0, of which 10 were built during the latter part of 1935 and were being delivered to the test centre at Rechlin for evaluation by the spring of 1936. Although inheriting the graceful lines of its single-engined predecessor, the He 70, and despite generally good handling characteristics, it was found that the BMW engines provided insufficient power for the He 111

to realise its desired performance. The similarly-powered He 111A-1s already completed were therefore rejected by the Luftwaffe, and the A-0s were sold to China. The DB 600A or C engine was chosen for the He 111B-0 and B-1, based on the He 111 V5 (D-APYS); deliveries of the B-1 began at the end of 1936, to KG 154, and these models were succeeded in 1937 by the He 111B-2 (950 hp DB 600CG), with a 1,500 kg (3,307 lb) internal bomb load over short ranges. Along with many other Luftwaffe types, the He 111B-2 was assigned to the Condor Legion in Spain at the beginning of 1937. It met with considerable success, acquiring a reputation of superiority over the opposition that was to prove, ultimately, something of a mixed blessing. In particular, the speed of the He 111 was such that, in Spain, it could outpace the opposing fighters and thus carry out unescorted raids with impunity. (The He 111D-1, with 950 hp DB 600Ga engines, was appreciably faster than the B-2, but only a few were built and these were not issued to operational units.) Continuation of its Spanish tactics in the face of the Spitfires and Hurricanes of 1940 had very different results, and before long the He 111 had to be given an increase in defensive armament and a fighter escort.

Aircraft type		He 111P-4	He 111H-16	He 111Z-1
Power plant		2 × 1,100 hp DB 601A-1	2 × 1,350 hp Jumo 211F-2	5 × 1,350 hp Jumo 211F-2
Accommodation		5	5	7
Wing span	m : ft in	22·60 : 74 1·8	22·60 : 74 1·8	35·20 : 115 5·8
Length overall	m : ft in	16·40 : 53 9·7	16·40 : 53 9·7	16·40 : 53 9·7
Height overall	m : ft in	4·00 : 13 1·5	4·00 : 13 1·5	4·00 : 13 1·5
Wing area	m² : sq ft	87·60 : 942·92	86·50 : 931·07	148·00 : 1,593·06
Weight empty equipped	kg : lb	8,015 : 17,670	8,680 : 19,136	21,500 : 47,399
Weight loaded (max)	kg : lb	13,500 : 29,762	14,000 : 30,865	28,600 : 63,052
Max wing loading	kg/m² : lb/sq ft	154·11 : 31·56	161·85 : 33·15	193·24 : 39·58
Max power loading	kg/hp : lb/hp	6·14 : 13·53	5·18 : 11·43	4·24 : 9·34
Max level speed	km/h : mph	322 : 200	405 : 252	435 : 270
at (height)	m : ft	5,000 : 16,405	6,000 : 19,685	6,000 : 19,685
Cruising speed	km/h : mph	311 : 193	355 : 221	364 : 226
at (height)	m : ft	5,000 : 16,405	5,000 : 16,405	5,800 : 19,030
Time to height		2,000 m (6,560 ft) in 14·2 min	2,000 m (6,560 ft) in 8·5 min	9,000 m (29,530 ft) in 30·0 min
Service ceiling	m : ft	4,500 : 14,765	6,700 : 21,980	9,600 : 31,495
Range (standard fuel)	km : miles	1,970 : 1,224	2,060 : 1,280	2,400 : 1,491

A total of 75 He 111Bs and Es served in Spain, and at the end of that war the 58 survivors became a part of the Spanish Air Force. Meanwhile, Heinkel had evolved a further civil series, the He 111G, which featured a simplified, straight-tapered wing instead of the more familiar semi-elliptical planform. Few customers were forthcoming, and production of the bomber models therefore continued with the He 111E. In order to preserve supplies of DB 600 engines for the fighter programme, the powerplant of the He 111E was changed to two Junkers Jumo 211A-1 engines of 1,010 hp each. Principal E models were the E-1 (2,000 kg; 4,409 lb internal bomb load), the E-3 (the most numerous), the E-4 (with 1,000 kg load internally and 1,000 kg externally), and the E-5 (with extra fuselage fuel tanks). The 1,100 hp Jumo 211A-3, plus the straight-tapered wing of the He 111G, were featured in the next bomber variant, the He 111F, which appeared in prototype form in the summer of 1937. Twenty-four He 111F-1s and five He 111G-5s were supplied to Turkey; the Luftwaffe F model was the He 111F-4.

About 90 He 111Js were built as torpedo-bombers, these being similar to the F-4 but with their bomb bays deleted and with DB 600CGs as their powerplant. In the event, however, they were delivered for standard bombing duties.

A new variant had begun to enter service, in the form of the He 111P, in the early months of 1939. This had a completely redesigned nose, with a continuous-curve contour (i.e. without a cockpit 'step') which not only improved the aerodynamics but also vastly enhanced the crew members' view. Extensively glazed, this new nose incorporated the offset-to-starboard, ball-type universal mount for the nose gun, a characteristic of all subsequent He 111s. The He 111P was powered by two 1,100 hp DB 601As; armament comprised three MG 15 machine-guns, and it could carry a maximum bomb load of 2,000 kg (4,409 lb). Half of this was made up of small bombs of up to 250 kg in size, still stowed vertically in the bomb bay, and the other half was carried externally.

A **Heinkel He 111** medium bomber (**GD + GW**), photographed from another during a test flight

Due partly to the need, once again, to reserve Daimler-Benz engines for fighter production, only about 400 He 111Ps were built, by Arado and Dornier as well as the parent company. Of these the P-1 and P-2 differed primarily in radio equipment only; the P-3 was a dual-control trainer conversion; the P-4 had armour protection for the crew and up to six MG 15 guns, plus (sometimes) an MG 17 in the tail; and the P-6 (the P-5 was not built) was the P-4 with 1,175 hp DB 601N engines. Ten P-6s were supplied to the Hungarian Air Force in 1942.

In May 1939 the Kampfgeschwadern began to receive the most widespread version of all, the He 111H. Except for having Jumo 211 engines instead of DB 601As, the early He 111Hs were generally similar to the P series. By the outbreak of World War 2, production of the He 111 had almost reached the 1,000 mark, of which the Luftwaffe had

Heinkel He 111P series bomber, which preceded the H series into production and service

Above: Heinkel He 111H-5 medium bombers on a wartime factory airfield. This version entered production in 1940

Above right: The He 111H-6, shown here dropping a 765 kg torpedo, was capable of carrying two of these weapons externally below the fuselage

Right: One of the major H variants was the **He 111H-16**, some of which were used by the Luftwaffe in a pathfinder role

A formation of **He 111P** bombers. This series were generally similar to the H series but were powered by DB 601 engines instead of Jumo 211s

in service 349 He 111Ps and 400 He 111Hs. The total number of He 111s built, before production ended in autumn 1944, was well in excess of 7,000, and more than 6,000 of these, covering a wide range of sub-types, were of the H series. Following their rough treatment by British fighters during the Battle of Britain, defensive armament had to be progressively strengthened, the number of crew members being increased to five or six accordingly. Two 7·9 mm beam guns were added on the He 111H-2; some anti-shipping H-3s were fitted with a 20 mm MG FF cannon in the under-nose gondola; the H-10 carried one MG FF, one MG 17 and one MG 131 or two MG 81s; the H-20 carried three MG 131s and four MG 81s. Successive models of the Jumo 211 engine powered most of the H series, although the H-21 and H-23 differed in having the 1,750 hp Jumo 213E and 1,776 hp Jumo 213A respectively. Principal members of the H series were the H-3, H-6 and H-16. The He 111H series were employed for a wide range of duties in various combat theatres, in addition to their medium bombing role, and carried a great variety of weapons and equipment. The He 111H-3 and H-6 became first-rate anti-shipping aircraft, the latter carrying bombs, mines or two external torpedos and entering operational service in the spring of 1942; the H-10 and H-18 were night bombers; the H-12 was modified to carry two Henschel Hs 293A glider-bombs; the H-14 was a pathfinder or glider tug; other H variants acted as air-launch platforms for Blohm und Voss glider-bombs (He 111H-15) or Fieseler Fi 103 flying bombs (He 111H-22); or as saboteur transports (He 111H-23). The He 111H-8 was fitted with a huge fender to push aside or cut through the cables of barrage balloons. More remarkable still was the He 111Z Zwilling (twin), a 'marriage' of two He 111H-6s, joined together by a new wing centre-section mounting a fifth Jumo engine and piloted from the port fuselage. This carried a crew of nine and was evolved in 1941–42 as a tug for the enormous Messerschmitt Me 321 Gigant trooping glider. The final H model to be built for the Luftwaffe was the H-23, an assault transport accommodating eight airborne troops.

The career of the He 111 did not end with the cessation of hostilities in Europe, for in 1941 the Spanish government had acquired a licence to build the He 111H-16 at the CASA plant at Tablada, under the Spanish designation C.2111. The Heinkel He 111's production life in Germany spanned nine years, and it remained in first-line service somewhere in the world for more than thirty years from the beginning of 1937.

The remarkable **He 111Z 'Zwilling'** (twin) in use as a glider tug for the Messerschmitt Me 321 Gigant

Heinkel He 114A-2 (IY + YK) two-seat reconnaissance floatplane

HEINKEL He 114

The He 114 was the less successful of two intended replacements for the He 60 shipboard reconnaissance aircraft, the other being the Ar 196. There were five variously engined prototypes (first flight spring 1936), and 10 He 114A-0s (880 hp BMW 132Dc) based on the V5. Weser then built 33 BMW 132N-engined A-1s for training and a small batch of operational A-2s. These had up-rated BMW 132Ks, one MG 17 (front) and one MG 15 (rear) guns, and could carry two 50 kg bombs. Flying and water handling qualities were poor; as a result the He 60 continued in service, Weser refurbishing most He 114A-2s pre-war for export to Sweden (14 as He 114B-1s) and Romania (12 as B-2s). Fourteen C-1s, with an extra MG 17 in front, were delivered to the Luftwaffe but released later to Romania, and four C-2s (unarmed A-2s) were exported, probably to Spain. The He 114's limited Luftwaffe service was mostly in the eastern Mediterranean and Black Sea areas. *Data : page 147.*

Aircraft type		He 115C-1
Power plant		2 × 960 hp BMW 132K
Accommodation		3
Wing span	m : ft in	22·28 : 73 1·2
Length overall	m : ft in	17·30 : 56 9·1
Height overall	m : ft in	6·62 : 21 8·6
Wing area	m² : sq ft	86·70 : 933·23
Weight empty equipped	kg : lb	6,870 : 15,146
Weight loaded (max)	kg : lb	10,680 : 23,545
Max wing loading	kg/m² : lb/sq ft	123·18 : 25·23
Max power loading	kg/hp : lb/hp	5·56 : 12·26
Max level speed	km/h : mph	300 : 186
at (height)	m : ft	1,000 : 3,280
Cruising speed (max)	km/h : mph	290 : 180
at (height)	m : ft	2,000 : 6,560
Time to 3,000 m (9,845 ft)		22·3 min
Service ceiling	m : ft	5,200 : 16,950
Range (normal)	km : miles	2,495 : 1,550

21
22
27
65
72
73

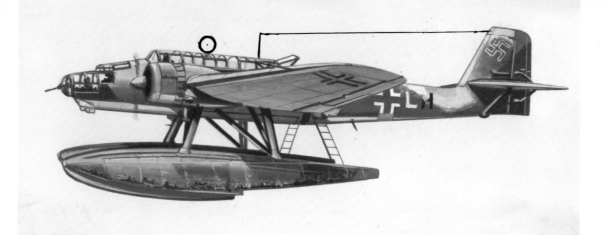

Above and below: Heinkel He 115B-1 (8L + LH) of 1./Kü Fl Gr 406, Norway, winter 1942/43

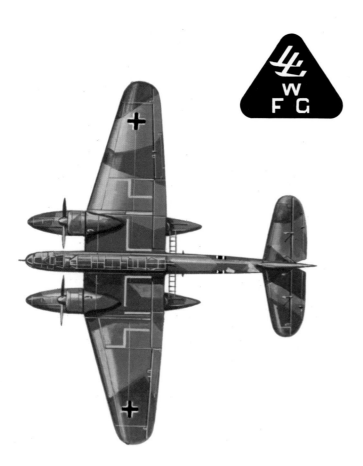

Staffel emblem of **2./Kü Fl Gr 506**, used also by **1./Kü Fl Gr 406**

Staffel emblem of **1./Kü Fl Gr 706**

HEINKEL He 115

One of the war's principal maritime reconnaissance and attack aircraft, the He 115 indicated its early promise on 20 March 1938 when the V1 (D-AEHF, first flown in August 1937 and later modified) captured eight international seaplane records in a single flight. By that time Heinkel had 10 pre-production He 115A-0s on the line, based on the V3 and V4, following them with 34 initial production A-1s or A-3s. Armed with two MG 15 machine-guns, one in the nose and one in the rear of the cockpit 'greenhouse', the A-1 was produced in parallel with the export A-2 for Norway (six) and Sweden (12). It entered Luftwaffe service in September 1939. The Weser-built B series (10 He 115B-0s and 18 B-1s/B-2s) carried extra fuel and an armament similar to the A-1. Offensive load comprised either five 250 kg bombs, one 500 kg bomb or torpedo, or one 920 kg or two 500 kg mines. During the early years of the war the robust and reliable He 115B was extremely active with various Küstenfliegergruppen, in minelaying and other forms of attack against Allied shipping in the English Channel, North Sea, Baltic and Arctic waters. Armament was increased by an under-nose 20 mm MG 151 cannon on the He 115C-0, C-1 and C-2,

which appeared in 1940–41; some of these aircraft also had an MG 17 in each wing root. A total of 76 Weser-built B and C series were completed by C-3 (minelayer) and C-4 (torpedo bomber) models, the latter having only a single dorsal MG 15 for defence. The sole He 115D was a converted A-1 with 1,600 hp BMW 801 MA engines, a fourth crew member, and an armament of one cannon and five machine-guns. This version did not enter production, but some existing He 115B/Cs were fitted with the 'chin' cannon during 1942–43, and others with an MG 81Z twin gun in the rear cockpit. The RAF gained two He 115A-2s which escaped from Norway in 1940, using them in the Mediterranean to ferry Allied agents between Malta and North Africa. The Luftwaffe also made limited use of the He 115 in the Mediterranean, but it had been phased out of first-line service by the end of 1944.

Heinkel He 115C-1 three-seat floatplane

HEINKEL He 162

One of the most rapidly conceived warplanes ever produced, the He 162 home defence fighter existed as a wooden mockup within 15 days of the issue, on 8 September 1944, of the RLM requirement. Seven days later a huge production contract was placed; detail design drawings were completed by the end of October; and on 6 December 1944—less than 13 weeks from initiation of the programme—the He 162 V1 (or A-01) made its first flight. Dubbed, for propaganda purposes, the Volksjäger or People's Fighter, the He 162 was of attractive if unorthodox appearance and was built largely of wood and other non-strategic materials. Its looks, how-

ever, belied a dangerous instability and some vicious handling characteristics, and troubles were also encountered (as in the Focke-Wulf Ta 154) with the wood-bonding adhesive used. Under the high priority given to fighter programmes in 1944–45, manufacture of the He 162, under the code name Salamander, was assigned to numerous factories. It was planned to produce 2,000 a month by May 1945 and 4,000 a month ultimately, and about 800 were in various stages of assembly when the war in Europe ended. A further 280 or so He 162A-0s, A-1s and A-2s had actually been completed. These differed primarily in their armament, the A-1 having two 30 mm MK 108 cannon in the lower forward fuselage and the A-2 a pair of 20 mm MG 151s.

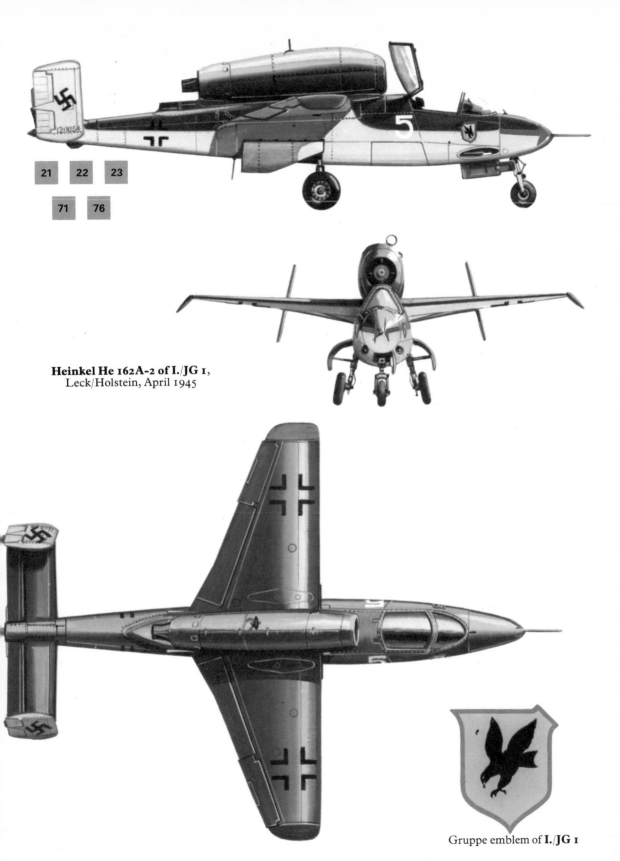

Heinkel He 162A-2 of I./JG 1,
Leck/Holstein, April 1945

| 21 | 22 | 23 |
| 71 | 76 | |

Gruppe emblem of **I./JG 1**

The first Luftwaffe unit to fly the He 162A was Erprobungs-kommando 162, which began to receive these aircraft in January 1945; but the first operational units, I. and II./ JG 1, were still working up at the beginning of May. Consequently, very few He 162s were actually encountered in combat. Proposed later versions included He 162A sub-types up to A-14, the He 162B (one or two pulse-jet engines), the He 162C (swept-forward wings), the He 162D (swept-back wings), and models with combined jet and rocket propulsion.

Aircraft type		He 162A-2
Power plant		1 × 800 kg (1,764 lb) st BMW 003E-1 or E-2
Accommodation		1
Wing span	m : ft in	7·20 : 23 7·5
Length overall	m : ft in	9·05 : 29 8·3
Height overall	m : ft in	2·60 : 8 6·4
Wing area	m² : sq ft	11·16 : 120·13
Weight empty	kg : lb	1,758 : 3,876
Weight loaded (max)	kg : lb	2,805 : 6,184
Max wing loading	kg/m² : lb/sq ft	251·34 : 51·48
Max power loading	kg/kg st : lb/lb st	3·51 : 3·51
Max level speed	km/h : mph	905 : 562
at (height)	m : ft	6,000 : 19,685
S/L rate of climb (max)	m/min : ft/min	1,406 : 4,613
Service ceiling	m : ft	12,000 : 39,370
Range (typical)	km : miles	*595–620 : 370–385

* at 6,000 m (19,685 ft)

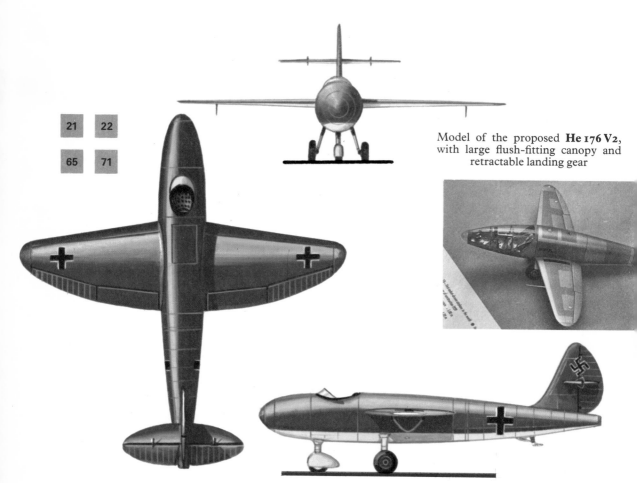

Model of the proposed **He 176 V2**, with large flush-fitting canopy and retractable landing gear

The **Heinkel He 176 V1**, which on 30 June 1939 became the world's first aeroplane to fly with a rocket engine

HEINKEL He 176 and He 178

The use of powder rockets for aircraft propulsion was explored in Germany in the late 1920s, but with little success. The first air tests with liquid-fuel rockets, developed by Hellmuth Walter and Wernher von Braun, took place respectively in autumn 1936 (on an He 72) and spring 1937 (using an He 112). Heinkel then initiated an aircraft specifically designed, by Hans Regner, for rocket propulsion. Two prototypes were planned. The He 176 V1, for low-speed trials with a Walter rocket motor, had a fixed tricycle landing gear, and an extremely slim fuselage with an open cockpit and a semi-reclining seat tailored literally to the test pilot, Flugkapitän Erich Warsitz. This made its first flight at Peenemünde on 20 June 1939, its second on the following day before senior RLM officials, and was demonstrated to Hitler at Rechlin in early July. Officially, however, the He 176 was regarded as little more than a dangerous toy, and approval was denied for the completion of the more advanced V2, which was to have conducted high-speed trials using a von Braun engine. The V2 would have had retractable main wheels, a streamlined flush-fitting canopy and a pilot escape system.

Meanwhile, in April 1936 Heinkel had engaged Dr Hans Joachim Pabst von Ohain and his colleague Max Hahn who, like Whittle in Britain, had been working privately on gas turbine engine development for some years. Their first demonstration engine was bench-tested in autumn 1937, and the developed HeS 3a was air-tested by the He 118 V2 in 1939. The He 178 was then designed around the 500 kg (1,102 lb) thrust HeS 3b engine, with which the He 178 V1 made a hop-flight at Marienehe on 24 August 1939 and its first true flight three days later. Subsequent demonstration to RLM officials in November (by then with the 590 kg; 1,301 lb st HeS 6) again brought little but scepticism, and the He 178 V2, although completed, was never flown. The RLM's policy at that time, also, was inclined to discourage non-engine manufacturers from dabbling in aero-engine development, particularly of turbojets; but in early 1940 Heinkel elicited sufficient interest to encourage him to proceed with the He 280 twin-jet fighter. The He 176 V1 and He 178 V1 were delivered to the Berlin Air Museum, where unfortunately they were destroyed by RAF bombs during 1943.

Aircraft type		He 176 V1	He 178 V1
Power plant		1 × 500 kg (1,102 lb) st Walter R I-203	1 × 450 kg (992 lb) st HeS 3b
Accommodation		1	1
Wing span	m : ft in	5·00 : 16 4·9	7·20 : 23 7·5
Length overall	m : ft in	5·20 : 17 0·7	7·48 : 24 6·5
Height overall	m : ft in	*2·10 : 6 10·7	2·10 : 6 10·7
Wing area	m² : sq ft	5·40 : 58·13	9·10 : 97·95
Weight empty	kg : lb	1,570 : 3,461	1,620 : 3,571
Weight loaded	kg : lb	2,000 : 4,409	1,998 : 4,405
Max wing loading	kg/m² : lb/sq ft	370·37 : 75·85	219·56 : 44·97
Max power loading	kg/kg st : lb/lb st	4·00 : 4·00	4·44 : 4·44
Max level speed	km/h : mph	700 : 435	632 : 393
at (height)	m : ft	S/L	S/L
Cruising speed	km/h : mph	— : —	580 : 360
at (height)	m : ft	— : —	S/L

* approx

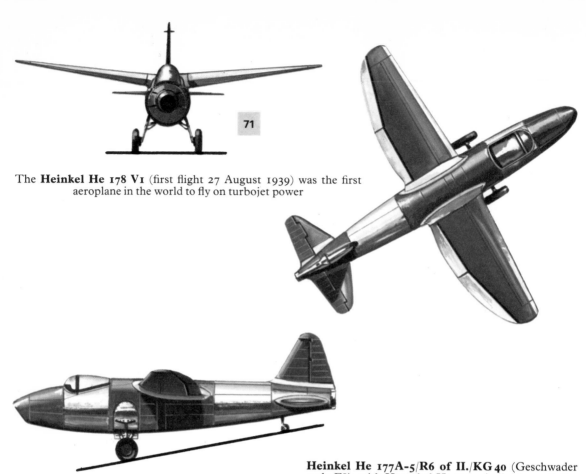

71

The **Heinkel He 178 V1** (first flight 27 August 1939) was the first
aeroplane in the world to fly on turbojet power

Heinkel He 177A-5/R6 of II./KG 40 (Geschwader
code F8), with Henschel Hs 293 missiles beneath the
fuselage and outer wings. This finish is one of several
applied to He 177s of this Gruppe engaged in anti-
shipping duties during 1943–44 from bases in the
Bordeaux-Mérignac area, and one for which there
appears to be no firm evidence of the application of
normal-style codes on the fuselage sides or beneath the
wings

HEINKEL He 177 GREIF (Griffin) and He 277

Had the He 177 been permitted a natural and uninterrupted development, it might have made a more effective contribution to the German war effort, for it was basically conventional in all but one aspect: the decision to employ two pairs of DB 605 engines, with each pair coupled as a DB 610 in a single nacelle and driving a single propeller. But official vacillation and political interference gave little chance for early faults to be overcome satisfactorily before it was pressed into service as Germany's only production wartime long-range strategic bomber. Designed to a 1938 requirement for a heavy bomber and anti-shipping aircraft, the He 177 V1, which first flew on 19 November 1939, was just within the gross weight specified, but production models became progressively heavier. More ominous, however, was the curtailment of the first flight due to engine overheating, a problem that remained with the He 177 for most of its career. The eight prototypes were followed by 35 pre-production He 177A-0s (built by Arado and Heinkel) and 130 Arado-built A-1s. Aircraft in this batch had DB 606 (coupled DB 601) engines. Some were allocated to various further trials, and after a brief and disastrous operational debut in mid-1942 the remainder were withdrawn from service. From late 1942 they were replaced by 170 Heinkel-built A-3s, and 826 examples of the A-5, which had a lengthened fuselage and the engine nacelles further out along the wing. Typical armament (of the He 177A-5/R7) comprised a 20 mm MG 151 cannon and two 7·9 mm MG 81 machine-guns, in front and rear of the under-nose gondola; one MG 81 in the nose; two 13 mm MG 131s in the forward dorsal barbette and one in the aft dorsal turret; and one MG 151 in the tail housing. Internal bomb load was 1,000 kg (2,205 lb), with external provision for carrying two mines, torpedos, or Hs 293A or FX 1400 guided missiles. The He 177A-3 and A-5 were employed chiefly by Kampfgruppen on the Eastern Front,

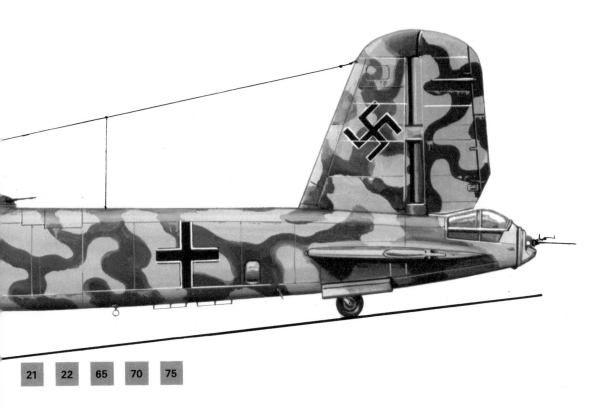

| 21 | 22 | 65 | 70 | 75 |

Aircraft type		He 177A-5/R2		
Power plant		2 × 2,950 hp DB 610A-1/B-1		
Accommodation		6		
Wing span	m : ft in	31·44 : 103	1·8
Length overall	m : ft in	22·00 : 72	2·1
Height overall	m : ft in	6·40 : 21	0·0
Wing area	m² : sq ft	102·00 : 1,097·92	
Weight empty equipped	kg : lb	16,800 : 37,038	
Weight loaded (max)	kg : lb	31,000 : 68,343	
Max wing loading	kg/m² : lb/sq ft	303·92 : 62·25	
Max power loading	kg/hp : lb/hp	5·25 : 11·58	
Max level speed	km/h : mph	440 : 273	
at (height)	m : ft	6,100 : 20,000	
Cruising speed (max)	km/h : mph	415 : 258	
at (height)	m : ft	6,100 : 20,000	
Time to 6,100 m (20,000 ft)		29·0 min	
Service ceiling	m : ft	8,000 : 26,245	
Range (max)	km : miles	*5,500 : 3,417	

* with two Hs 293s

The **Heinkel He 177 V8 (SF + TC)** had a gross weight of 27,910 kg (61,531 lb), compared with the 23,920 kg (52,735 lb) of the V1. Weight escalation remained one of the He 177's major problems, the A-5 attaining a gross weight nearly 15 per cent greater than that of the original design estimate

where their use also for ground attack resulted in various alternative armaments, including the use of 50 mm and 75 mm cannon. Apart from conversion of six A-5s to He 177A-6s and six to A-7s, attention then concentrated on versions of the bomber with four separately-mounted engines. These included the He 274A (originally the He 177A-4) and the He 277, a converted He 177A-3 to which Heinkel gave the false designation 'He 177B' to evade official disapproval of this re-engined version. The prototype He 274A was still awaiting its first flight at Farman's Surèsnes factory when German forces evacuated Paris. The He 277 did fly, in late 1943, with four 1,730 hp DB 603A engines, and was followed by two more prototypes and a few production aircraft; but the latter did not enter squadron service.

HEINKEL He 219 UHU (Owl)

Although expressing little interest in the multi-purpose aircraft Projekt 1060 when first submitted in mid-1940, the RLM had decided by late 1941 that it was worthy of being pursued if developed for night fighting, and the He 219 V1 made its first flight on 15 November 1942, powered by two 1,750 hp DB 603A engines. The He 219 proved to be fast and manoeuvrable, was well armed and equipped with Lichtenstein radar, and an order was quickly placed for 100 aircraft. Despite destruction of most of the design drawings in an RAF raid in March 1943, this order was trebled by April, when deliveries began to I./NJG 1 of some 20 pre-production He 219A-0s. Many of these were modified by Rüstsätze (field conversion kits) which added various ventral gun packs or upward-firing dorsal Schräge Musik cannon installations. In mid-June 1943 the He 219 made a sensational debut when one of I./NJG 1's aircraft destroyed five RAF Lancasters during a single half-hour sortie; but its prime value was that it could compete on equal terms with the escorting Mosquito fighters. From late 1943 the A-0 was followed by the two-seat He 219A-2 (only a few A-1s were built). The proposed three-seat A-3 bomber and high-altitude reconnaissance A-4 were not adopted, production continuing with the A-5, the A-6 and the major service version, the A-7. Most of these were powered by variants of the DB 603 engine, but Jumo 213Es were installed in the A-7/R5 and Jumo 222s in the A-7/R6. The guns varied, a typical example being that of the He 219A-5/R2, with two 20 mm MG 151 cannon in the ventral pack, two above the fuselage in the Schräge Musik installation and two others in the wing roots. Total A-series production amounted to 268 and only these, together with some 20 prototypes or pre-production examples plus a few two-seat He 219B-2s (an extended-span version, developed from the A-6) served operationally with the Luftwaffe. The He 219 was widely regarded as the best-equipped night fighter of World War 2, and it was fortunate for the Allies that RLM procrastination prevented more from being produced. Thanks to cancellation and counter-cancellation in 1944, the only other unit to equip fully with the He 219 was NJGr 10, an experimental anti-Mosquito unit, although elements of other units also received the type. Prototypes were completed of the He 219C-1 night fighter and C-2 fighter-bomber (to carry three 500 kg bombs); but when the war ended these were still awaiting delivery of their Jumo 222 engines.

Heinkel He 219A-5/R1 two-seat night fighter, with Lichtenstein C-1 and SN-2 radar arrays mounted on the nose

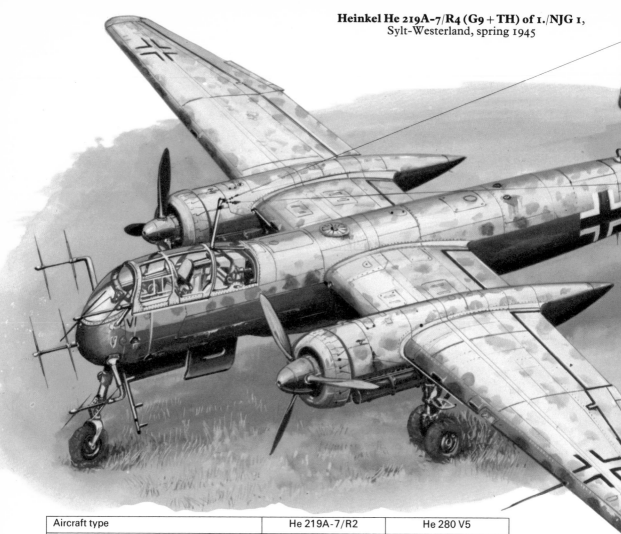

Aircraft type		He 219A-7/R2	He 280 V5
Power plant		2 × 1,800 hp DB 603E	2 × 800 kg (1,764 lb) st BMW 003A Sturm
Accommodation		2	1
Wing span	m : ft in	18·50 : 60 8·3	12·20 : 40 0·3
Length overall	m : ft in	16·34 : 53 7·3	10·40 : 34 1·4
Height overall	m : ft in	4·10 : 13 5·4	3·06 : 10 0·5
Wing area	m² : sq ft	44·50 : 478·99	21·50 : 231·42
Weight empty	kg : lb	9,205 : 20,293	3,055 : 6,735
Weight loaded (max)	kg : lb	15,100 : 33,290	4,400 : 9,700
Max wing loading	kg/m² : lb/sq ft	339·33 : 69·50	204·65 : 41·91
Max power loading	kg/hp or lb/hp or kg/kg st : lb/lb st	4·19 : 9·25	2·75 : 2·75
Max level speed	km/h : mph	585 : 363	820 : 509
at (height)	m : ft	6,000 : 19,685	6,000 : 19,685
Cruising speed (max)	km/h : mph	510 : 317	— : —
at (height)	m : ft	6,000 : 19,685	— : —
S/L rate of climb	m/min : ft/min	600 : 1,968	1,146 : 3,760
Service ceiling	m : ft	9,800 : 32,150	11,500 : 37,730
Range	km : miles	2,000 : 1,243	970 : 603

21

22

74

75

77

Above: Heinkel He 280 V2 (GJ + CA) in the summer of 1942, after refitting with Jumo 004 engines and arming with three 20 mm MG 151 cannon

Right: A rare in-flight photograph of one of the **He 280** prototypes, probably the V1

The **Heinkel He 280 V1 (DL + AS)** taking off for its first flight on 2 April 1941

HEINKEL He 280

The first jet aircraft in the world to be designed as a fighter, the He 280 V1 (DL + AS) flew for the first time under power on 2 April 1941, with two of von Ohain's 500 kg (1,102 lb) st Heinkel HeS 8A (109-001) centrifugal turbojets. Although the V2, V3 and V5 were similarly powered, this engine failed to produce the expected 750 kg (1,653 lb) of thrust, and in 1943 the V2 was re-engined with more powerful Jumo 004s; the V4 flew with BMW 003s; and the V5 also was fitted with BMWs. Nine prototypes had flown by the end of August 1943, the V6 and V9 having BMWs and the V7 and V8 having Jumos. The He 280 showed excellent promise, exhibiting a performance superior to both the Fw 190 and the Me 262. For example, the He 280 V5, at 4,300 kg (9,480 lb) gross weight and armed with three 20 mm MG 151 cannon in the nose, had a sustained maximum speed of 820 km/h (510 mph) at 6,000 m (19,685 ft), a sea-level rate of climb of 1,146 m (3,760 ft)/min, and a service ceiling of 11,500 m (37,730 ft), even with the HeS 8A engines. The Me 262, however, had better armament and range, and was eventually preferred, with the consequent abandonment of the proposed He 280A and B production fighters. The prototypes continued to be used as development aircraft in aerodynamic and powerplant research programmes. The V1 and V4, for instance, were flown with Argus pulse-jets (four and six respectively); the V7 had its engines removed and was flown as a glider in a wing efficiency research programme; and the V8 was fitted with a Vee tail that yielded data used in the design of the He 162.

HENSCHEL Hs 123

Though supposedly obsolete by 1939, the Luftwaffe's last combat biplane (it had entered service in mid-1936) continued to find steady work not only in the early Polish, French and Russian campaigns but right through to mid-1944 with various close support Schlachtgruppen; even then the survivors performed such useful second-line roles as glider towing or supply dropping. In its first-line role the Hs 123 established a commendable reputation, both for pin-point accuracy of attack and for ability to withstand battle damage, and its lack of radio in no way inhibited the excellent support given to the ground forces. The Hs 123 V1 first flew in the spring of 1935, two of the first three prototypes breaking up during high-speed diving tests, but the production Hs 123A-1, based on the strengthened V4 and having an uprated engine, successfully overcame the early problems. The decision to standardise on the Ju 87 for the dive-bomber role, plus considerable success as a close support aircraft during the Spanish Civil War, led to the Hs 123A-1 being re-allocated to the latter type of duty. In addition to an armament of two 7.9 mm MG 17 machine-guns above the engine, it could be equipped with a pair of 20 mm MG FF cannon, four 50 kg bombs, or canisters with ninety-two 2 kg anti-personnel bombs beneath the lower wings. Production of the Hs 123A-1, which ended in the autumn of 1938, was about 60: comparatively small by contemporary German standards. The proposed pre-war Hs 123B (960 hp BMW 132K) and ground attack Hs 123C did not enter production.

Henschel Hs 123A-1 (PF + UV) of Schlacht Training Gruppe attached to **II.(S)/LG 2**, Novotsucherkask (Rostov), late 1941

Aircraft type			Hs 123A-1
Power plant			1 × 880 hp BMW 132Dc
Accommodation			1
Wing span	m	: ft in	10·50 : 34 5·4
Length overall	m	: ft in	8·33 : 27 4·0
Height overall	m	: ft in	3·21 : 10 6·4
Wing area	m²	: sq ft	24·85 : 267·48
Weight empty	kg	: lb	1,504 : 3,316
Weight loaded (normal)	kg	: lb	2,215 : 4,883
Wing loading	kg/m²	: lb/sq ft	89·13 : 18·25
Power loading	kg/hp	: lb/hp	2·52 : 5·55
Max level speed	km/h	: mph	341 : 212
at (height)	m	: ft	1,200 : 3,935
Cruising speed (max)	km/h	: mph	317 : 197
at (height)	m	: ft	2,000 : 6,560
S/L rate of climb	m/min	: ft/min	900 : 2,953
Service ceiling	m	: ft	9,000 : 29,525
Range (max)	km	: miles	860 : 534

Gruppe emblem of **5.II.(S)/LG 2**

HENSCHEL Hs 124

Evolved for the RLM's 1934 Kampfzerstörer requirement, the Hs 124 was abandoned after this programme was split into separate Zerstörer and Schnellbomber (high-speed bomber) requirements. There were three prototypes, all of which should have been powered by DB 600 engines, but these were not available soon enough. Instead, the V1 (first flight spring 1936) was powered by two 600 hp Junkers Jumo 210C inverted-Vee engines, and the V2 by 880 hp BMW 132Dc radials. The V1's intended armament com-

The radial-engined **V2** second prototype of the **Henschel Hs 124**

prised a 20 mm MG 151 cannon in a power-operated nose turret and a single movable 7·9 mm MG 15 gun in the rear cockpit. However, the turret also was not available for early tests. The V1 therefore flew with a mockup turret, while the V2 had a completely redesigned, fully-glazed nose, eliminating the turret altogether in favour of a pair of gimbal-mounted cannon to be operated by the bomb-aimer. The V3 was intended to have two 20 mm MG FF cannon and two 7·9 mm MG 17s in a 'solid' nose. The internal bomb bay of the Hs 124 was designed to hold six 100 kg bombs; alternatively, this space could be used for additional fuel storage, in which case eight 50 kg bombs could be attached to an under-fuselage rack and two more under each wing. *Data: page 147.*

HENSCHEL Hs 126

The Hs 126 reconnaissance and Army co-operation aircraft, although most effective when aerial opposition was scarce, could often give a surprisingly good account of itself—as in November 1941, when three Greek Henschels strafed a 4½-mile Italian armoured column. Based on the earlier Hs 122, the Jumo-powered Hs 126 V1 (a converted Hs 122A-0) first flew in the autumn of 1936. Ten pre-production A-0s, based on the Hs 126 V3 and having Bramo 323 radials, were delivered for service trials in the winter of 1937/38, followed in the spring by the first BMW 132-engined Hs 126A-1s. Armament comprised two 7·9 mm guns—an MG 17 in front and a movable MG 15 in the rear cockpit—and ten 10 kg bombs could be accommodated in the rear camera bay, with a single 50 kg bomb attached below the base of the port wing struts. Pre-war deliveries included 16 Hs 126A-1s to Greece and six to Spain. The Hs 126B-1 entered production in mid-1939, and by the outbreak of World War 2 there were some 275 A-1/B-1s in service with 10 Luftwaffe Aufklärungsgruppen. When production ended in January 1941 about 800 Hs 126s had been built, and at the start of the Russian campaign five months later about half that number were in service with nearly 50 Army co-operation units. In this theatre the Hs 126 began increasingly to need fighter protection, and from the following spring was phased out in favour of the Fw 189. Thereafter it was used for glider towing, or with the Nachtschlachtgruppen on night 'nuisance' raids against partisan groups in the Balkans.

Henschel Hs 126B-1 (4E + EL) of 3.(H)/13,
France, May/June 1940

Aircraft type			Hs 126B-1
Power plant			1 × 850 hp BMW-Bramo 323A-1 or Q-1
Accommodation			2
Wing span	m	: ft in	14·50 : 47 6·9
Length overall	m	: ft in	10·85 : 35 7·2
Height overall	m	: ft in	3·75 : 12 3·6
Wing area	m²	: sq ft	31·60 : 340·14
Weight empty	kg	: lb	2,032 : 4,480
Weight loaded (max)	kg	: lb	3,270 : 7,209
Max wing loading	kg/m²	: lb/sq ft	103·48 : 21·19
Max power loading	kg/hp	: lb/hp	3·85 : 8·48
Max level speed	km/h	: mph	355 : 221
at (height)	m	: ft	3,000 : 9,845
Cruising speed	km/h	: mph	300 : 186
at (height)	m	: ft	4,000 : 13,125
Time to 6,000 m (19,685 ft)			12·7 min
Service ceiling	m	: ft	8,230 : 27,000
Range (max)	km	: miles	*720 : 447

* at 4,200 m (13,780 ft)

HENSCHEL Hs 128 and Hs 130

Two prototypes of the 26·00 m (85 ft 3·6 in) span Hs 128 were flown in 1939, as high altitude research aircraft powered by two supercharged DB 601 (in the V1) or Jumo 210 (V2) engines. Equipped with a two-seat pressurised shell in the cabin, they reached heights of up to 12,000 m (39,370 ft) and prompted the Luftwaffe to seek a developed version for reconnaissance. This emerged as the Hs 130, of which three prototypes were flown in 1940, similar to the Hs 128 except for reduced wing span, retractable landing gear, DB 601R engines with GM-1 power boost, and two remote-control cameras in

Henschel Hs 130E-0 (CF + OZ) pressurised high altitude reconnaissance aircraft

the rear fuselage. Seven Hs 130A-0s followed from early 1941, five of 25·50 m (83 ft 7·9 in) span and two of 29·00 m (95 ft 1·7 in) with DB 605Bs. Neither the Hs 130B proposed bomber nor the Hs 130D was produced, the latter's complex supercharging system being discarded in favour of the HZ-Anlage system of the Hs 130E, in which a DB 605T in the fuselage drove a huge blower to supercharge the two DB 603B propulsion engines. Flown in late 1942, the Hs 130E V1 and V2 (and later the V3) reached heights of up to 15,000 m (49,215 ft) with

the HZ-Anlage operating, and seven E-0s were to have been followed by 100 E-1s; but this order was subsequently cancelled, and the four-engined Hs 130F project (BMW 801TJs) was abandoned. Odd man out was the Hs 130C, a total redesign with a four-seat, glazed pressure cabin, remotely controlled armament and much larger fuselage. Three prototypes were flown in 1942–43 to compete with the Do 317, Fw 191 and Ju 288 bombers, but production plans for 100 or more Hs 130C-1s were abandoned. *Data : page 147.*

HENSCHEL Hs 129

The 1937 RLM specification that resulted in the Hs 129 was prompted by the need, revealed during the Spanish Civil War, for a specialised close support and ground attack aeroplane. Dipl-Ing Friedrich Nicolaus of Henschel based his design on the use of two 465 hp Argus As 410A-1 engines, and the Hs 129 V1 was flown in the spring of 1939. Eight pre-series A-0s were built for service trials in 1940 but pilots' reports were so unfavourable (mainly due to the lack of power and cockpit view) that the Argus-engined Hs 129A did not enter production. Nicolaus proposed an alternative design (Projekt P.76), but this was rejected by the RLM, which ruled instead that the Hs 129A design be adapted to accept captured French

Gnome-Rhône radial engines. With cockpit and other interior modifications, this version became the Hs 129B. Ten pre-series B-0s were followed into production in March 1942 by the Hs 129B-1, which became operational with Luftwaffe units in the Crimea in early 1942. Later, the Hs 129B appeared in quantity in North Africa, being employed in both theatres primarily in an anti-tank role. Several B-1 sub-types appeared, with various alternative armaments. Standard installation, as in the B-1/R1, comprised two 20 mm MG 151 cannon and two 7·9 mm MG 17 machine-guns, with provision for an external load of two 50 kg or forty-eight 2 kg bombs. Without bombs, and with a fixed ventral 30 mm MK 101 cannon added, it was designated B-1/R2; the B-1/R3 had the large cannon replaced by a ventral tray of four

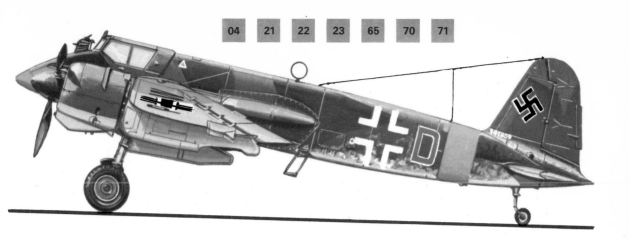

04 21 22 23 65 70 71

Henschel Hs 129B-2/R2 of 4./Sch G 1, Eastern Front, summer 1943

Aircraft type		Hs 129B-2
Power plant		2 × 700 hp Gnome-Rhône 14M 4/5
Accommodation		1
Wing span	m : ft in	14·20 : 46 7·1
Length overall	m : ft in	9·75 : 31 11·9
Height overall	m : ft in	3·25 : 10 8·0
Wing area	m² : sq ft	29·00 : 312·15
Weight empty equipped	kg : lb	4,020 : 8,863
Weight loaded (max)	kg : lb	5,250 : 11,574
Max wing loading	kg/m² : lb/sq ft	181·03 : 37·08
Max power loading	kg/hp : lb/hp	3·75 : 8·27
Max level speed	km/h : mph	407 : 253
at (height)	m : ft	3,830 : 12,565
Cruising speed	km/h : mph	315 : 196
at (height)	m : ft	3,000 : 9,845
Time to 3,000 m (9,845 ft)		7·0 min
Service ceiling	m : ft	9,000 : 29,525
Range	km : miles	690 : 429

Inboard profile showing the ventral installation of a 30 mm MK 103 cannon on the **Hs 129B-2/R2**

MG 17s; the B-1/R4 and R5 each combined the standard B-1 gun installation with a heavier bomb load (R4) or reconnaissance camera (R5). The B-1/R2, particularly successful as an anti-tank aircraft, prompted the all-gun Hs 129B-2 series. The B-2/R1 was similar to the B-1/R1, but with 13mm MG131s replacing the two nose MG17s; the B-2/R2 added a 30mm MK 103 cannon; the B-2/R3 mounted four MG 151s in the nose and a 37mm BK 3·7 underneath; and the B-2/R4 and B-3 each carried a huge 75mm BK 7·5 ventral cannon whose muzzle projected nearly 8ft (2·44m) beyond the nose. Among other weapons tested were rocket projectiles and flame-throwers. All versions had extensive armour protection of the forward fuselage and cockpit, but the pilot's view remained poor and the French engines were far from trouble-free. Production ended in September 1944 after the completion of 869 aircraft, including three prototypes and 848 Hs 129Bs.

Photographed at Travemünde in May 1944, this **Hs 129B-2** (Werk Nummer 141258) was fitted with a mockup of the 75 mm BK 7·5 cannon installation for aerodynamic testing. About 24 Hs 129B-3s were fitted with this anti-tank weapon, which could fire a 12 kg shell. In an emergency, the entire installation could be jettisoned

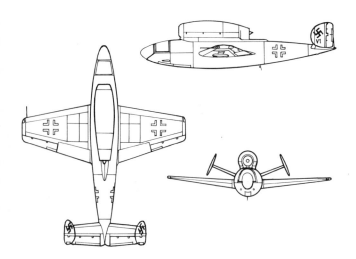

To help the pilot withstand the high physical strains anticipated when using the **Hs 132** as a dive-bomber, Henschel designed the cockpit with a prone piloting position behind a fully transparent nose cap. It was considered that the Hs 132, with its high speed and small frontal area, would make a difficult target for anti-aircraft gunners

HENSCHEL Hs 132

Despite its similarity of appearance to the He 162 Volksjäger, the Hs 132 was intended for dive-bombing and ground attack, and was to make extensive use of non-strategic materials, notably in the wings, which were largely of wooden construction. The pilot was to lay prone in the well-glazed nose, and a single 500 kg bomb was to be attached under the fuselage. Planned armament comprised two under-nose 20 mm MG 151s in the Hs 132A (dive-bomber) and the Jumo 004-engined Hs 132B (ground attack); the

Hs 132C (Hirth 011 engine) was to have the option of two extra guns (30 mm MK 103s) or a larger (1,000 kg) bomb; and the Hs 132D an enlarged wing. Of six prototypes ordered, the V1 was scheduled to fly in June 1945, with the V2 (also an A-series prototype) and the V3 (first of four B-series prototypes) shortly afterwards. The V4 to V6 were also in the final assembly stage when Henschel's Schönefeld factory was captured by Soviet forces; whether any prototypes were eventually completed and/or flown is unknown. *Data: page 147.*

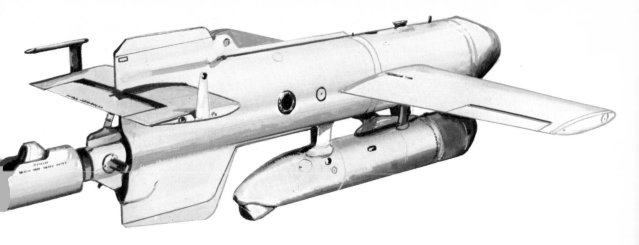

76

Henschel Hs 293A. These missiles were normally painted overall in the underside colour (usually 65 or 76) of the carrier aircraft. See also the He 177 painting on pages 84–85

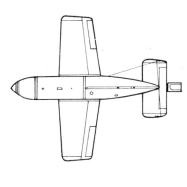

Aircraft type			Hs 293A-1
Power plant			1 × 600 kg (1,323 lb) st HWK 109-507B
Wing span	m	: ft in	3·10 : 10 2·0
Length overall	m	: ft in	3·82 : 12 6·4
Body diameter	m	: ft in	0·47 : 1 6·5
Wing area	m²	: sq ft	1·92 : 20·67
Weight of warhead	kg	: lb	295 : 650
Launch weight	kg	: lb	1,045 : 2,304
Max wing loading	kg/m²	: lb/sq ft	544·27 : 111·49
Max power loading	kg/kg st	: lb/lb st	1·74 : 1·74
Max speed	km/h	: mph	435–900 : 270–559
Launch altitude	m	: ft	400–2,000 : 1,310–6,560
Range	km	: miles	3·5–18 : 2·2–11·2

HENSCHEL Hs 293

Serious missile development at Henschel, under Prof Dr Herbert Wagner, began in 1939, primarily to evolve an air-to-surface weapon for use against shipping and land-based targets. Preliminary testing of the Hs293 glider-bomb began in 1940, leading to the first flight of a pre-series Hs 293A-0 on 16 December 1940. ('Pre-series' is a rather misleading term here, since about 1,700 of the first 1,900 built were development A-0s.) The basic ingredients of the production weapon were the warhead of a 500 kg HE bomb; a pair of stub-wings; a rear fuselage with tail surfaces; and an underslung pod containing the liquid-fuel rocket engine. Telefunken and Stassfurter provided the radio guidance systems, which were installed in the rear fuselage.

The Hs293A-1 production version was air-launched at medium or low altitudes from such carrier aircraft as the Do217, Fw200, He177 and Ju290, and underwent its service evaluation, prior to use by the Kampfgeschwadern, by Lehr- und Erprobungskommando 36, a special unit formed for the purpose in July 1943. After launch, the motor was fired for 10 seconds, to speed it ahead of, but still in line-of-sight of, the control aircraft, from which it was guided on to its target. The Hs293A-1 was first launched in anger, from a Do217E of II./KG 100, on 25 August 1943, and during the next 12 months was deployed extensively in day and night attacks from the Atlantic to the Mediterranean. Thereafter its use was more restricted, but continued until as late as April 1945.

Several developed versions were tested or proposed, including the TV-guided Hs293D; the delta-winged Hs293F, with twin 1,855 kg (4,090 lb) st Schmidding SG33 solid-fuel rockets; the gyro-actuated Hs 293G, which could attack almost vertically or horizontally; and the Hs293H, intended to explode in the midst of a bomber formation either on receipt of a radio control signal or by means of a proximity fuse. Twin-engined variations included the Hs294, with a long, conical nose and enlarged wings; the Hs295, with Hs293 rear fuselage, Hs294 wings and a larger warhead; and the Hs296, with Hs294 wings and rear fuselage and an alternative enlarged warhead.

JUNKERS W 33 and W 34

The W33 and W34 were pre-war transport aircraft developed from the earlier F13 and powered, respectively, by an in-line or radial engine. Both flew for the first time in 1926, the W33 subsequently reaching a production total of 199 and the W34 a total of 1,791. A reconnaissance/light bomber export version of the W34 was designated K43. Normal powerplant of the W33 series was a Junkers L5 engine; various W34 models appeared, mostly with Siemens Sh20, BMW-Bramo 322, BMW 132, Armstrong Siddeley Panther, or Bristol Jupiter or Mercury engines. Accommodation in both types was for six people, and either type could have wheel, ski or twin-float landing gear. In addition to extensive pre-war airline service, both types found early employment by the still-clandestine Luftwaffe for communications, patrol and training. Many W34s and, to a lesser extent, W33s continued to serve on such duties until the end of World War 2. At least eight wartime FFS are known to have operated W34s, as did several Transportstaffeln; a few were also employed by the early Störkampfstaffeln as 'harassment' aircraft in early 1943. Foreign operators of the W34 included the air forces of Croatia, Finland, Romania, Slovakia and Sweden. *Data: page 147.*

Junkers W 34hau (CA + VC) communications and training aircraft. The long-chord cowling of the 650 hp Bramo 322 engine was a characteristic of this version

One of the two giant **Junkers G 38** 'flying wing' transports, built for DLH in the early 1930s, survived to don Luftwaffe livery as **GF + GG** in September 1939. It was operated by **KGrzbV 172** in Norway before being destroyed in May 1941 during an RAF air attack on Athens

Junkers Ju 52/3m g6e floatplane of **Seetransportstaffel 1**, Crete, 1941

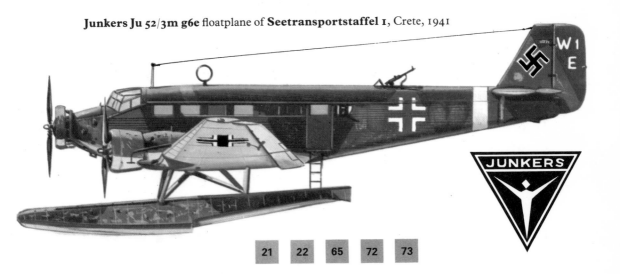

| 21 | 22 | 65 | 72 | 73 |

JUNKERS Ju 52/3m

Junkers' universally known 'Tante Ju' (Auntie Ju) or 'Iron Annie', designed by Dipl-Ing Ernst Zindel, originated in 1928 with the single-engined Ju 52 which first flew on 13 October 1930, powered by an 800 hp Junkers L 88 Vee-type engine. Six months later, Junkers flew the first example of a tri-motor version of this aircraft, the Ju 52/3m, powered by three 575 hp BMW-built Pratt & Whitney Hornet radial engines. It entered production in 1934, and was soon in widespread commercial use with DLH and various foreign airlines. In the same year it was also adopted for use by the military, several hundred being built initially as interim four-seat bombers for the embryo Luftwaffe, following the failure of the Dornier Do 11. The first major bomber version, the Ju 52/3m g3e, entered service in the summer of 1936, when 20 were among the first combat aircraft despatched by Germany to support the Nationalist forces in the Spanish Civil War. By the end of 1937, however, the Ju 52/3m had been largely superseded in the bomber role with the Luftwaffe by more modern types such as the Do 17, He 111 and Ju 86, and was instead performing the more appropriate role of troop and supply transport for which it was later to become world-famous. The semi-retractable ventral 'dustbin', mounting a 7·9 mm MG 15 machine-gun, was generally omitted from these early transports, although

Junkers Ju 52/3m g4e (MS) (NJ + NH) of Minensuchgruppe 1, *ca* 1942

Aircraft type			Ju 52/3m g7e
Power plant			3 × 830 hp BMW 132T-2
Accommodation			3 + 17
Wing span	m	: ft in	29·25 : 95 11·6
Length overall	m	: ft in	18·90 : 62 0·1
Height overall	m	: ft in	5·55 : 18 2·5
Wing area	m²	: sq ft	110·50 : 1,189·41
Weight empty	kg	: lb	6,500 : 14,330
Weight loaded (max)	kg	: lb	11,000 : 24,251
Max wing loading	kg/m²	: lb/sq ft	99·55 : 20·39
Max power loading	kg/hp	: lb/hp	4·42 : 9·74
Max level speed	km/h	: mph	286 : 178
at (height)	m	: ft	1,400 : 4,595
Cruising speed (max)	km/h	: mph	253 : 157
at (height)	m	: ft	1,400 : 4,595
Time to 3,000 m (9,845 ft)			17·5 min
Service ceiling	m	: ft	5,900 : 19,355
Range (standard fuel)	km	: miles	1,100 : 683

they retained the single MG 15 installed in an open dorsal position to provide rearward defence. Following the g3e (725 hp BMW 132A-3 engines) came successive military variants distinguished by suffixes from g4e to g14e, which signified either the specific role of a particular model (transport, ambulance, mine clearance etc), the installation of successive variants of the BMW 132 engine (a licence-built version of the Hornet), or miscellaneous structural alterations. The Ju 52/3m g5e, for example, had 830 hp BMW 132T-2 engines, while the g9e had the BMW 132Z

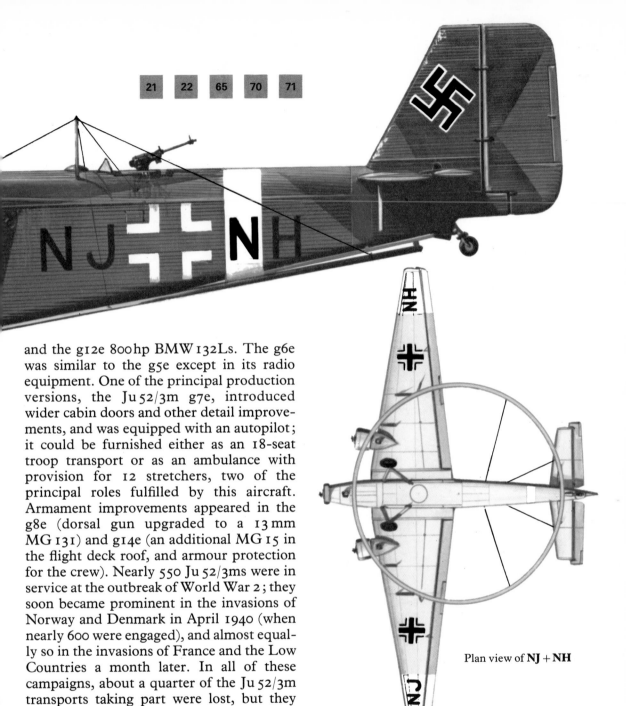

21 22 65 70 71

and the g12e 800hp BMW 132Ls. The g6e was similar to the g5e except in its radio equipment. One of the principal production versions, the Ju 52/3m g7e, introduced wider cabin doors and other detail improvements, and was equipped with an autopilot; it could be furnished either as an 18-seat troop transport or as an ambulance with provision for 12 stretchers, two of the principal roles fulfilled by this aircraft. Armament improvements appeared in the g8e (dorsal gun upgraded to a 13 mm MG 131) and g14e (an additional MG 15 in the flight deck roof, and armour protection for the crew). Nearly 550 Ju 52/3ms were in service at the outbreak of World War 2; they soon became prominent in the invasions of Norway and Denmark in April 1940 (when nearly 600 were engaged), and almost equally so in the invasions of France and the Low Countries a month later. In all of these campaigns, about a quarter of the Ju 52/3m transports taking part were lost, but they continued to play a major part in subsequent years in the assaults on the Eastern Front, in the Balkans, North Africa and, particularly, Crete, despite a continuing high rate of attrition. Production of the Ju 52/3m was to continue in Germany until July 1944, the overall number built—including civil examples plus wartime batches built in France (361), Hungary (26) and Spain (70)—

Plan view of **NJ + NH**

eventually reaching approximately 4,850. Their versatility was enhanced by the ability to operate from wheel, ski or twin-float landing gear. Proposed replacements, the Ju 252 and Ju 352, failed to materialise in quantity, and the Ju 52/3m instead soldiered on until long after the end of World War 2.

Right: This photograph of a group of export **Ju 86Ks** awaiting delivery illustrates the pre-war appearance of this bomber/transport

Below: Junkers Ju 86P Vı (D-AUHB, a converted Ju 86D), early 1940. This aircraft still has the pre-war splinter camouflage, officially superseded in 1938 by the black-green 70/dark green 71 two-colour pattern

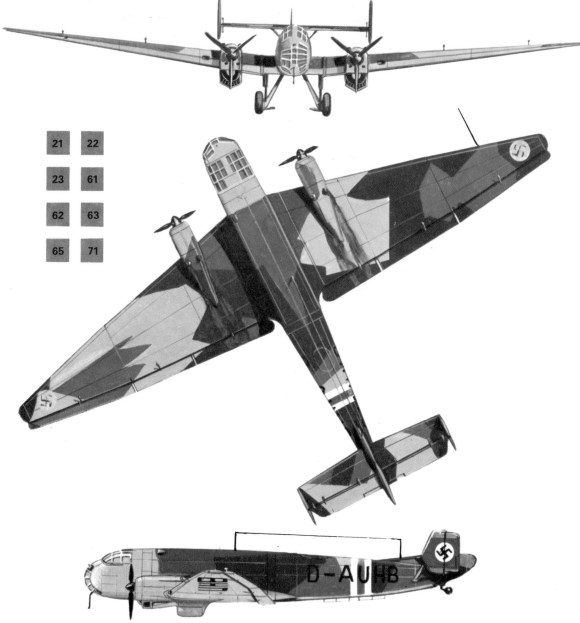

Aircraft type		Ju 86P-1
Power plant		2 × 950 hp Jumo 207A-1
Accommodation		2
Wing span	m : ft in	25·60 : 83 11·9
Length overall	m : ft in	16·46 : 54 0·0
Height overall	m : ft in	4·70 : 15 5·0
Wing area	m² : sq ft	92·00 : 990·28
Weight empty	kg : lb	6,660 : 14,683
Weight loaded	kg : lb	10,400 : 22,928
Max wing loading	kg/m² : lb/sq ft	113·04 : 23·15
Max power loading	kg/hp : lb/hp	5·47 : 12·07
Max level speed	km/h : mph	360 : 224
at (height)	m : ft	6,000 : 19,685
Cruising speed	km/h : mph	260 : 162
at (height)	m : ft	11,000 : 36,090
Time to 11,000 m (36,090 ft)		45·0 min
Service ceiling	m : ft	12,000 : 39,370
Range (normal)	km : miles	1,000 : 621

JUNKERS Ju 86

Designed in 1934 to a joint specification for a DLH commercial transport and Luftwaffe bomber, the Ju 86 first flew on 4 November 1934. Nearly 50 were in pre-war commercial service, including 17 Ju 86Z-7s later taken over by the South African Air Force. The bomber prototypes were followed in early 1936 by 13 pre-series Ju 86A-0s for service trials, and initial deliveries of about 20 Ju 86A-1s were made to KG 152 (later KG 1) in May 1936, these having 600 hp Jumo 205C-4 engines and an 800 kg (1,764 lb) internal bomb load. Next bomber version

was the D-1, with increased fuel and a lengthened rear fuselage, before a powerplant change to 810 or 865 hp BMW 132F or N engines was introduced on the Ju 86E-1 and E-2, about 50 of which began to enter service in late summer 1937. The Ju 86G (40 built) was the E with a redesigned forward fuselage, and there were 235 A/D/E/G models in service by the autumn of 1938. By the outbreak of war these had been virtually replaced in all Luftwaffe bomber units by the Do 17 and He 111, although sales of Ju 86K series bombers had been made to Chile, Hungary, Portugal, South Africa and Sweden. The Ju 86P-1 and P-2 were high altitude bomber and photographic reconnaissance conversions of the Ju 86D with a shorter, redesigned glazed nose, increased wing span and Jumo 207A engines. Over Britain, the USSR and North Africa in 1940–42, the unarmed Ju 86P could fly high enough to be almost immune from interception; but by 1942 they were no longer safe from all Allied fighters. The Ju 86R-1 and R-2, with a further increase in span to 32·00m (104ft 11·8in) and boosted Jumo 207Bs, could fly even higher, but only a few were converted (from Ps), and they were little used.

JUNKERS Ju 87

Design of the Ju 87 dive-bomber and ground attack aircraft, by Dipl-Ing Pohlmann, began in 1933, and the Ju 87 V1 prototype first flew in early 1935. This was powered by a Rolls-Royce Kestrel engine and had twin rectangular fins and rudders, but the Ju 87 V2, flown in autumn 1935, was more representative of the production version, having a 610 hp Jumo 210A engine and a single tail. Following a 1936 pre-series batch

of Ju 87A-0s, deliveries began in spring 1937 of the Ju 87A-1 and the generally similar A-2. About 200 A-series were built before, in autumn 1938, there appeared the much-modified, Jumo 211-powered Ju 87B, with enlarged vertical tail, redesigned cockpit enclosure and new-style fairings over the main-wheel legs instead of the earlier 'trousered' type. Both A and B models were active with the Luftwaffe's Condor Legion in the Spanish Civil War, but by September 1939 the Ju 87As had been re-deployed as train-

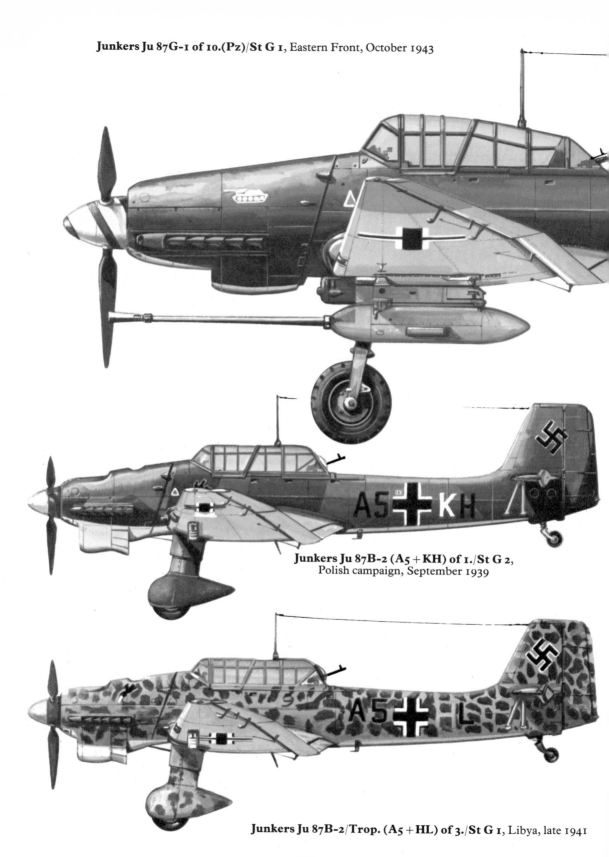

Junkers Ju 87G-1 of 10.(Pz)/St G 1, Eastern Front, October 1943

Junkers Ju 87B-2 (A5 + KH) of 1./St G 2,
Polish campaign, September 1939

Junkers Ju 87B-2/Trop. (A5 + HL) of 3./St G 1, Libya, late 1941

21 22 24 27 65

70 71 78 79 80

Emblem of **10.(Pz)/St G 1**

Junkers Ju 87B dive-bomber, probably in Greece

Gruppe emblem of **I./St G 1**

Junkers Ju 87D-1/Trop. (S7 + AA) of St G 3, Libya, June 1942 (aircraft of the Geschwaderkommodore, Oberstleutnant Walter Sigel)

Aircraft type			Ju 87A-1	Ju 87B-2	Ju 87D-1
Power plant			1 × 600 hp Jumo 210Ca	1 × 1,200 hp Jumo 211Da	1 × 1,400 hp Jumo 211J-1
Accommodation			2	2	2
Wing span	m	: ft in	13·80 : 45 3·3	13·80 : 45 3·3	14·70 : 48 2·7
Length overall	m	: ft in	10·83 : 35 6·4	11·10 : 36 5·0	11·30 : 37 0·9
Height overall	m	: ft in	3·90 : 12 9·5	4·01 : 13 1·9	3·90 : 12 9·5
Wing area	m²	: sq ft	31·90 : 343·37	31·90 : 343·37	33·60 : 361·67
Weight empty equipped	kg	: lb	2,315 : 5,104	3,900 : 6,085	3,900 : 8,598
Weight loaded (max)	kg	: lb	3,400 : 7,496	4,250 : 9,370	6,600 : 14,551
Max wing loading	kg/m²	: lb/sq ft	106·58 : 21·83	133·23 : 27·29	196·43 : 40·23
Max power loading	kg/hp	: lb/hp	5·31 : 11·71	3·54 : 7·81	4·71 : 10·39
Max level speed	km/h	: mph	295 : 183	380 : 236	410 : 255
at (height)	m	: ft	3,000 : 9,845	4,100 : 13,450	4,100 : 13,450
Cruising speed (max)	km/h	: mph	275 : 171	336 : 209	318 : 198
at (height)	m	: ft	2,700 : 8,860	3,700 : 12,140	5,100 : 16,730
Time to height			3,000 m (9,845 ft) in 23·0 min	3,700 m (12,140 ft) in 12·0 min	5,000 m (16,405 ft) in 19·8 min
Service ceiling	m	: ft	7,000 : 22,965	8,000 : 26,245	7,300 : 23,950
Range (max)	km	: miles	1,000 : 621	*595 : 370	1,535 : 954

* with 500 kg bomb

ers, leaving a first-line strength of 336 as dive-bombers, all Ju 87B-1s. Their ugly lines and wailing engines struck an especial note of terror throughout their comparatively uninterrupted attacks on Poland, France and the Low Countries during 1939–40, but against sterner opposition during the Battle of Britain their losses mounted rapidly. Despite this, Ju 87B production continued into 1941, including substantial numbers for the Bulgarian, Hungarian, Italian and Romanian air forces; and the Ju 87B continued to perform effectively in Luftwaffe service in the Mediterranean, the Balkans, North Africa and Russia, where Germany still maintained some measure of air superiority. In parallel production was the Ju 87R, which from 1940 was employed for anti-shipping and other duties. The pre-war Ju 87C, a 'navalised' version of the B with arrester hook and folding wings, was planned for the aircraft carrier *Graf Zeppelin* which, in the event, was never completed; instead, the few Ju 87C-0s built served with a land-based unit, and others begun as C-1s were completed as B-2s. Several sub-types were built of the next major series, the Ju 87D. This had a cleaned-up airframe, uprated Jumo engine, armour protection, and increased armament and fuel. Most Ds were ground attack models, with weapon loads ranging from a single 1,800 kg under-fuselage bomb to a pair of underwing pods each with six 7·9 mm machine-guns. The Ju 87D-5 introduced an extended wing of 15·00 m (49 ft 2·6 in) span; the D-7 was a more specialised version for ground attack at night. Final operational variants were the anti-tank Ju 87G, developed from the D-5, and the Ju 87H dual-control combat trainer, produced by converting various Ju 87D sub-types. The Ju 87G, which entered service in 1943, carried a 37 mm BK 3·7 cannon in a streamlined fairing beneath each wing, with which it became quite successful at knocking out Soviet tanks until better-class Soviet fighters got the measure of it after the autumn of 1944. Production ended in September 1944, when more than 5,700 Ju 87s (all models) had been built.

JUNKERS Ju 88

The most versatile German combat aircraft of World War 2, and among the most widely used, the Ju 88 was evolved to a 1935 RLM requirement for a three-seat Schnellbomber

Aircraft type		Ju 88A-4	Ju 88C-6c	Ju 88G-7b
Power plant		2 × 1,340 hp Jumo 211J-1	2 × 1,340 hp Jumo 211J-1	2 × 1,725 hp Jumo 213E
Accommodation		4	3	4
Wing span	m : ft in	20·00 : 65 7·4	20·00 : 65 7·4	20·00 : 65 7·4
Length overall	m : ft in	14·40 : 47 2·9	14·36 : 47 1·4	16·36 : 53 8·1
Height overall	m : ft in	4·85 : 15 10·9	5·07 : 16 7·6	4·85 : 15 10·9
Wing area	m² : sq ft	54·50 : 586·63	54·50 : 586·63	54·50 : 586·63
Weight empty equipped	kg : lb	9,860 : 21,738	9,060 : 19,974	9,300 : 20,503
Weight loaded (max)	kg : lb	14,000 : 30,865	12,350 : 27,227	14,675 : 32,353
Max wing loading	kg/m² : lb/sq ft	256·88 : 52·61	226·61 : 46·41	269·27 : 55·15
Max power loading	kg/hp : lb/hp	5·18 : 11·43	4·57 : 10·08	4·25 : 9·38
Max level speed	km/h : mph	470 : 292	495 : 307	626 : 389
at (height)	m : ft	5,300 : 17,390	5,300 : 17,390	9,100 : 29,855
Cruising speed	km/h : mph	400 : 248	423 : 263	560 : 348
at (height)	m : ft	5,000 : 16,405	6,000 : 19,685	9,000 : 29,530
Time to height		5,400 m (17,715 ft) in 23·0 min	6,000 m (19,685 ft) in 12·7 min	9,200 m (30,185 ft) in 26·4 min
Service ceiling	m : ft	8,200 : 26,905	9,900 : 32,480	10,000 : 32,810
Range (standard fuel)	km : miles	1,790 : 1,112	1,040 : 646	2,250 : 1,398

Junkers Ju 88A, showing the hinged rear portion of the ventral gondola (including the MG 15 gun) lowered to provide access for the crew. The two internal bomb bays were immediately aft of this position

(high-speed bomber). The Ju 88 V1 first prototype (D-AQEN) flew for the first time on 21 December 1936, powered by two 1,000 hp DB 600Aa engines. The V2 was similar, but the Jumo 211 was substituted in the Ju 88 V3, and this engine powered the majority of Ju 88s subsequently built; the characteristic multi-panelled glazed nose first appeared on the four-seat V4. Following 10 pre-series Ju 88A-os completed in mid-1939, deliveries of the Ju 88A-1, based on the V6, began in the following August. The A series continued, with very few gaps, through to the A-17, and included variants for such diverse roles as dive-bombing, anti-shipping strike, long-range reconnaissance and conversion training. Probably the most common model was the Ju 88A-4, which served in Europe and North Africa. This was the first version to incorporate modifications from experience gained in the Battle of Britain: it had extended-span wings, Jumo 211J engines, a 1,500 kg (3,307 lb) bomb load and increased defensive armament. Twenty-three Ju 88A-4s were supplied to Finland in 1943, 52 A-4s and D-1s to the Regia Aeronautica, and other A-4s to the Romanian Air Force. In parallel with the Ju 88A bomber series, Junkers pursued development of the basic airframe as a

Junkers Ju 88A-4/Trop. (L1 + FN)
of 5./LG 1, Libya, 1942

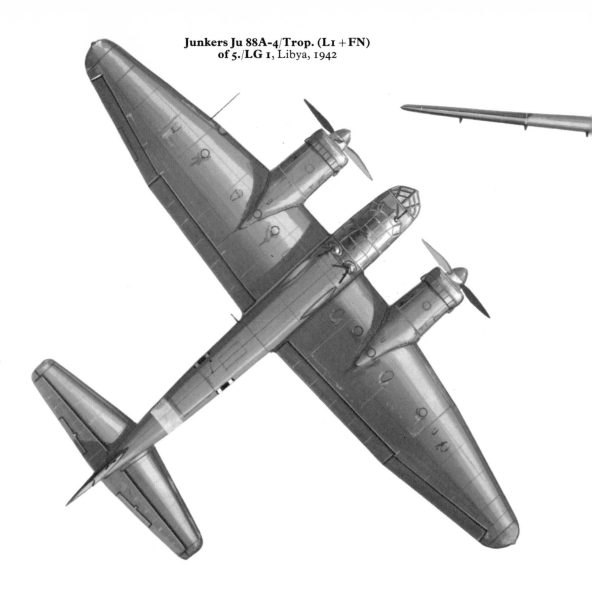

Junkers Ju 88G-6c (4R + BR) of 7./NJG 2 (aircraft of the Staffelkapitän, Oberleutnant W. Briegleb), Luftflotte
Reich, winter 1944/45

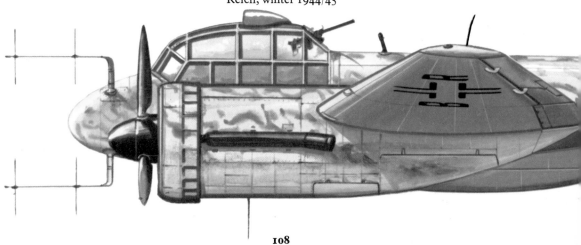

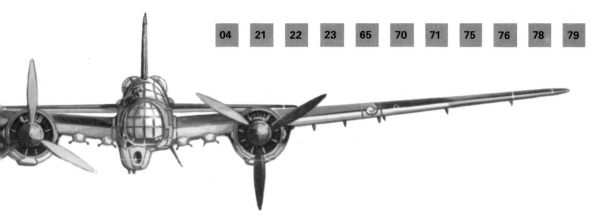

04 21 22 23 65 70 71 75 76 78 79

Above and below: Junkers Ju 88A-4 (5K + VN) of 5./KG 3 'Blitz',
northern USSR, summer 1941

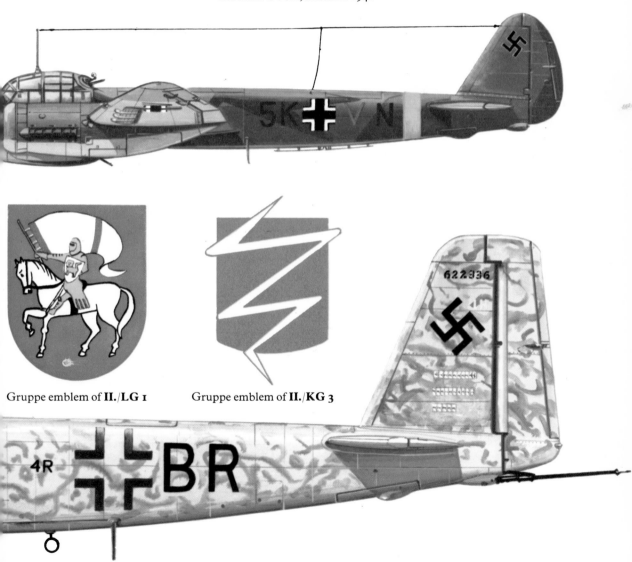

Gruppe emblem of **II./LG 1**

Gruppe emblem of **II./KG 3**

'heavy' fighter, or Zerstörer, for which its speed and sturdy construction made it particularly suitable. This emerged as the Ju 88C (the pre-war Ju 88B having followed a separate course to become the Ju 188), and the first such model was the Ju 88C-2, a few conversions of the Ju 88A-1 with a 'solid' nose mounting three 7·9 mm MG 17 machine-guns and a 20 mm MG FF cannon, plus two aft-firing MG 15 guns. The C-2 entered service with II./NJG 1 in July 1940, being followed by small batches of the C-4 (with the A-4's extended-span wings) and the C-5 (BMW 801D engines). Armament was improved in the C-6, the first major fighter version, powered by Jumo 211J engines and having (in the C-6b) Lichtenstein BC or C-1 radar. Final C sub-type was the C-7 which, like the C-6, operated both as a Zerstörer and as a night fighter. The Ju 88D series, of which nearly 1,500 were built, were developed versions of the Ju 88A-4 for the strategic reconnaissance role; they, too, were used by the Hungarian and Romanian air forces. Night fighter developments continued with the Ju 88G, which utilised the angular vertical tail of the Ju 188 bomber and carried the improved Lichtenstein SN-2 radar. The G series appeared from spring 1944, principal sub-types being the G-1 and

G-4 (BMW 801D engines), G-6a and G-6b (BMW 801G), G-6c (Jumo 213A), and G-7 (Jumo 213E). Small batches were built of the Ju 88H-1 (long-range reconnaissance) and H-2 (Zerstörer). A specialised version, produced primarily for service on the Eastern Front, was the Ju 88P. This was a ground attack/anti-tank aircraft with a 'solid' nose and either a 75 mm PaK 40 cannon (in the P-1), two 37 mm BK 3·7 cannon (in the P-2 and P-3), or a 50 mm BK 5 cannon (in the P-4) mounted in a ventral pack. Next bomber series was the Ju 88S, produced in three small sub-series as the S-1 (BMW 801G), S-2 (BMW 801TJ) and S-3 (Jumo 213A). The S series, which entered service in autumn 1943, differed from earlier bomber models in having a smaller, fully-rounded glazed nose. They were only lightly armed, but offered considerably better performance than the Ju 88A and D series. Bomb load varied from 910 kg (2,006 lb) internally to 2,000 kg (4,409 lb) externally. The Ju 88T-1 and T-3 were photo-reconnaissance counterparts of the S-1 and S-3, introduced in early 1944. Towards the end of the war, many Ju 88s ended their days as explosive-laden lower portions of Misteln composite attack weapons, carrying a Bf 109 or Fw 190 fighter on

Junkers Ju 290A-5 in markings typical of **2./FAGr 5**, *ca* winter 1943/44. (Individual aircraft codes not confirmed)

their backs to guide them to their targets. Production, which ended in 1945, included more than 8,800 bombers, about 3,950 fighters and about 1,900 reconnaissance variants, overall output (excluding prototypes) reaching 14,676—built, in addition to Junkers, by Arado, Dornier, Heinkel, Henschel and Volkswagen factories.

JUNKERS Ju 90, Ju 290 and Ju 390

Based on the Ju 89 bomber, the Ju 90 transport (first flown on 28 August 1937) was used commercially by DLH from 1938 until taken over by the Luftwaffe in 1940, when some were employed in the invasion of Norway. Several Ju 90s became prototypes

Aircraft type			Ju 90B-1	Ju 290A-5	*Ju 390A-1
Power plant			4 × 880 hp BMW 132H	4 × 1,700 hp BMW 801D	6 × 1,970 hp BMW 801E
Accommodation			4 + 40	9	6
Wing span	m	: ft in	35·02 : 114 10·7	42·00 : 137 9·5	50·30 : 165 0·3
Length overall	m	: ft in	26·30 : 86 3·4	28·64 : 93 11·6	34·20 : 112 2·5
Height overall	m	: ft in	7·50 : 24 7·3	6·83 : 22 4·9	6·90 : 22 7·7
Wing area	m²	: sq ft	184·00 : 1,980·56	203·60 : 2,191·53	253·60 : 2,729·73
Weight empty	kg	: lb	16,000 : 35,274	33,000 : 72,753	36,900 : 81,351
Weight loaded	kg	: lb	23,000 : 50,706	44,970 : 99,142	75,500 : 166,449
Max wing loading	kg/m²	: lb/sq ft	125·00 : 25·60	220·87 : 45·24	297·71 : 60·98
Max power loading	kg/hp	: lb/hp	6·53 : 14·41	6·61 : 14·58	6·39 : 14·08
Max level speed	km/h	: mph	350 : 217	440 : 273	505 : 314
at (height)	m	: ft	2,500 : 8,200	6,000 : 19,685	7,050 : 23,130
Cruising speed	km/h	: mph	320 : 199	360 : 224	358 : 222
at (height)	m	: ft	3,000 : 9,845	2,000 : 6,560	2,500 : 8,200
Time to height			1,000 m (3,280 ft) in 4·2 min	1,850 m (6,070 ft) in 9·8 min	— : —
Service ceiling	m	: ft	5,500 : 18,045	6,000 : 19,685	— : —
Range (standard fuel)	km	: miles	1,250 : 777	6,150 : 3,821	9,700 : 6,027

* weights and performance estimated

21 22 23 65 72 73

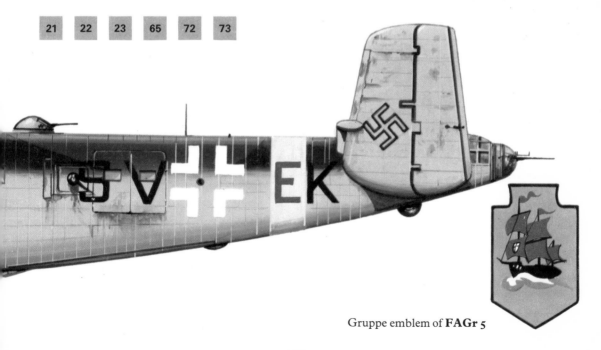

Gruppe emblem of **FAGr 5**

The **Ju 90 V5** (formerly **D-ABDG Württemberg** of DLH) was also the first production **Ju 90B-1**. Seen here without national markings, it was later used in the development programme for the Ju 290 (originally Ju 90S) for the Luftwaffe

for the Ju 290 military derivative, of which about 65 were built, including five Ju 290A-1s, three A-2s, three A-3s, five A-4s, 29 A-5s, about 12 A-7s and one A-8. These differed mainly in armament and fuel load, and entered service from early 1943, operating at first with FAGr 5 on long-range maritime patrol over the Atlantic from their base in occupied France. From mid-1944 most Ju 290s were transferred to I./KG 200, a special unit performing agent-dropping and similar duties. The Ju 290 had from the outset been fitted with a hydraulically-operated rear-loading ramp known as a Trapoklappe, and the single Ju 290A-6, built as a 50-passenger transport, served with Hitler's personal transport unit, the Führer-

kurierstaffel. One example of the Ju 290B-1 was built, as a prototype pressurised high altitude bomber, and in 1943 two prototypes of the larger Ju 390, a six-engined heavy bomber/reconnaissance aircraft with an estimated range of 9,700 km (6,027 miles). The Ju 390 V2 underwent operational trials with FAGr 5 in early 1944, including one test flight to within 20 km (12 miles) of New York.

JUNKERS Ju 188

This descendant of the Ju 88 first flew in late 1942, the prototypes being modified Ju 88s with pointed wingtips, square-cut vertical tails and BMW 801MA engines. Jumo

Aircraft type			Ju 188A-2	Ju 188E-1
Power plant			2 × 1,776 hp Jumo 213A-1	2 × 1,700 hp BMW 801D-2
Accommodation			4	4
Wing span	m	: ft in	22·00 : 71 2·1	22·00 : 72 2·1
Length overall	m	: ft in	14·95 : 49 0·6	14·95 : 49 0·6
Height overall	m	: ft in	4·45 : 14 7·2	4·45 : 14 7·2
Wing area	m²	: sq ft	56·00 : 602·78	56·00 : 602·78
Weight empty equipped	kg	: lb	9,900 : 21,826	9,860 : 21,738
Weight loaded	kg	: lb	14,500 : 31,967	14,510 : 31,989
Max wing loading	kg/m²	: lb/sq ft	258·93 : 53·03	259·11 : 53·07
Max power loading	kg/hp	: lb/hp	4·08 : 9·00	4·27 : 9·41
Max level speed	km/h	: mph	520 : 323	500 : 311
at (height)	m	: ft	6,000 : 19,685	6,000 : 19,685
Cruising speed	km/h	: mph	400 : 249	375 : 233
at (height)	m	: ft	6,000 : 19,685	5,000 : 16,405
Time to 6,100 m (20,015 ft)			20·0 min	17·6 min
Service ceiling	m	: ft	9,500 : 31,170	9,350 : 30,675
Range	km	: miles	*2,400 : 1,491	**1,950 : 1,212

* with 1,500 kg (3,307 lb) bomb load   ** with 2,000 kg (4,409 lb) bomb load

213A-1s powered the Ju 188A-0, A-2 and A-3, the A-3 having Hohentwiel radar and carrying two 800 kg torpedos underwing. The A models were preceded by the Ju 188E series (BMW 801s), comprising the E-0, E-1 and torpedo-bomber E-2; the E-1 entered service in mid-1943. The other major series, representing more than half of the 1,100 or so Ju 188s built, were the Jumo-engined Ju 188D-1 and D-2, and the Ju 188F-1 and F-2 with BMW 801s. All of these were basically reconnaissance variants, and were employed widely with Aufklärungsgruppen on the Eastern and Western Fronts and in Italy. The projected C and G (bomber) and H and M (reconnaissance) series did not enter production, and the Ju 188J, K and L were developed separately as the Ju 388J, K and L. The Ju 188R, modified from the E, was an experimental night fighter; the Ju 188S-1 and T-1 were respectively unarmed intruder and reconnaissance versions with Jumo 213E-1 engines, redesigned forward fuselages, and cabins pressurised for high-altitude flight. The Ju 188S-1/U armoured close-support version mounted a 50 mm BK 5 cannon in an under-fuselage fairing.

Junkers Ju 188E-1 of I./KG 66
in 'pathfinder' colour scheme,
Rennes, March 1944

JUNKERS Ju 252 and Ju 352 HERKULES (Hercules)

Intended for DLH, to succeed the Ju 52/3m, the pressurised Ju 252 instead became a freight and special-duty Luftwaffe transport, serving with LTS 290, TS 5 and I./KG 200 during 1943–44. Only 15 were built: four prototypes (first flight October 1941) and 11 Ju 252A-1s, the latter with a 13 mm MG 131 machine-gun in a dorsal turret. Instead of projected B, C and D series, Junkers developed the Ju 352 Herkules (first flight 1 October 1943), using fewer strategic materials. The 45 built included two prototypes, 10 Ju 352A-0s and 33 A-1s. They were delivered from spring 1944, serving with I./KG 200 and the Ju 352 Gruppe as special-duty and supply transports until 1945. *Data : page 147.*

The civil-registered **Ju 252 V1 (D-ADCC)**, which first flew in late October 1941

Junkers Ju 352A (TH + JB) transport, showing the Trapoklappe hydraulically operated rear loading ramp lowered

JUNKERS Ju 287

The studies leading to this radical jet bomber began in 1943 by a Junkers team under Dipl-Ing Hans Wocke, and support from Oberst Siegfried Kneymeyer, head of the Luftwaffe's Technical Air Armament department, resulted in a prototype contract in March 1944. Its then-unique forward-swept wings were allied to a modified He 177A fuselage and tail surfaces from a Ju 388, the resulting Ju 287 V1 (RS + RA) flying for the first time on

Aircraft type			Ju 287 V1
Power plant			4 × 900 kg (1,984 lb) st Jumo 004B-1 Orkan
Accommodation			2
Wing span	m	: ft in	20·116 : 66 0·0
Length overall	m	: ft in	18·28 : 59 11·7
Height overall (approx)	m	: ft in	5·40 : 17 8·6
Wing area	m²	: sq ft	58·30 : 627·54
Weight empty	kg	: lb	12,500 : 27,558
Weight loaded	kg	: lb	20,000 : 44,092
Max wing loading	kg/m²	: lb/sq ft	343·05 : 70·26
Max power loading	kg/kg st	: lb/lb st	5·55 : 5·55
Max level speed	km/h	: mph	559 : 347
at (height)	m	: ft	6,000 : 19,685
Cruising speed (max)	km/h	: mph	512 : 318
at (height)	m	: ft	7,000 : 22,965
Service ceiling	m	: ft	10,800 : 35,435
Range (max)	km	: miles	1,500 : 932

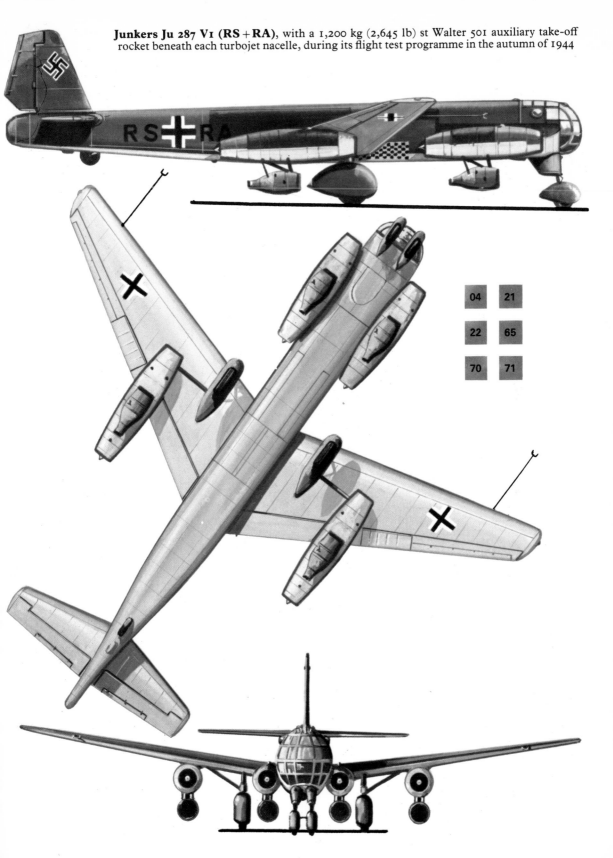

Junkers Ju 287 V1 (RS + RA), with a 1,200 kg (2,645 lb) st Walter 501 auxiliary take-off rocket beneath each turbojet nacelle, during its flight test programme in the autumn of 1944

04	21
22	65
70	71

16 August 1944. This aircraft, built for low-speed trials, had a non-retractable tricycle landing gear. Development of bombers was suspended in summer 1944 in favour of fighters, but in early 1945 that of the Ju 287 was resumed. The modified V2 and V3, however, with six BMW 003A-1 engines, remained uncompleted at the war's end, and the planned Ju 287A and B production series were never built. The A-0, based on the V3, was to have had a three-seat pressurised crew cabin, a 4,000 kg (8,818 lb) internal bomb load, and two 13 mm MG 131 guns in a remotely-controlled tail barbette. The Ju 287 V1, which had made 17 flights, was captured at Rechlin by advancing Soviet forces and taken to the USSR for further flight testing; the V2, also captured, was completed in Russia with swept-back wings and test flown with various powerplants during 1947–48.

JUNKERS Ju 288

Favoured entrant for the 'Bomber B' competition of 1939, the elegant Ju 288 was Junkers' official contender for a Ju 88 replacement, but suffered many development setbacks, including engine supply problems, and the entire programme was cancelled in mid-1943 after 21 prototypes had been completed. These were for production series designated Ju 288A (V1 to V5), Ju 288B (V6 to V9 and V11 to V14) and Ju 288C (V101 to V108), with various BMW, Daimler-Benz or Junkers Jumo engines, differing combinations of remotely-controlled armament, and a 3,000 kg (6,614 lb) internal bomb load.

The **V103** was the first **Ju 288C** prototype to be fitted with DB 610 'double' engines

First flight was in January 1941; a few later served with operational units. *Data: page 147.*

Aircraft type		Ju 388J-1	Ju 388L-1
Power plant		2 × 1,800 hp BMW 801TJ	2 × 1,800 hp BMW 801TJ
Accommodation		4	3
Wing span	m : ft in	22·00 : 72 2·1	22·00 : 72 2·1
Length overall	m : ft in	17·70 : 58 0·9	15·20 : 49 10·4
Height overall	m : ft in	4·34 : 14 2·9	4·34 : 14 2·9
Wing area	m² : sq ft	56·00 : 602·78	56·00 : 602·78
Weight empty	kg : lb	10,400 : 22,928	10,345 : 22,806
Weight loaded	kg : lb	14,675 : 32,353	14,675 : 32,353
Max wing loading	kg/m² : lb/sq ft	262·05 : 53·67	262·05 : 53·67
Max power loading	kg/hp : lb/hp	4·08 : 8·99	4·08 : 8·99
Max level speed	km/h : mph	583 : 362	616 : 383
at (height)	m : ft	12,300 : 40,355	12,280 : 40,290
Time to height		8,000 m (26,245 ft) in 21·0 min	11,000 m (36,090 ft) in 30·0 min
Service ceiling	m : ft	13,000 : 42,650	13,440 : 44,095
Range	km : miles	*1,010 : 1,625	**3,475 : 2,159

* typical   ** max with auxiliary tank

02

21

22

70

71

76

Prototype for the K series high altitude bomber was the **Ju 388 V3**, which first flew in January 1944 and had a short-range bomb load of 3,000 kg (6,614 lb)

Junkers Ju 388L-1 (RT+KE), fitted with an FA 15 barbette in the tail which housed a pair of remotely controlled 13 mm MG 131 machineguns. Two cameras and an auxiliary fuel tank were installed in the ventral pannier

JUNKERS Ju 388

Despite the priority afforded to it in autumn 1943, only the Ju 388L photo-reconnaissance version of this high-altitude multipurpose development of the Ju 188S and T saw any operational service, and even that was limited. Based on the Ju 388L V1 (a converted Ju 188T-1, first flown in late 1943), 10 pre-series Ju 388L-os were built by Allgemeine Transportanlagen GmbH (ATG) and 45 Ju 388L-1s by ATG and Weser. Service trials with the L-os were conducted, from August 1944, by EKdo 388, and the L-1 later entered service with the Versuchsverbänd ob d L. The specified

Junkers Ju 388 V2 with Lichtenstein SN-2 radar array, early 1944

Junkers Ju 388L-1 in typical factory finish, autumn 1944

standard armament for all Ju 388s was a remotely-controlled tail barbette mounting two 13 mm MG 131 machine-guns, but protracted development and delayed deliveries of this installation caused the L-0 to be fitted instead with a ventral fairing with two rearward-firing 7·9 mm MG 81s. The L-1 had the tail barbette; a few were converted to L-1/b with a third MG 131 in the rear of the cockpit; and there were two L-3s with 1,750 hp Jumo 213E-1 engines. There were three prototypes (V2, V4 and V5) for the proposed Ju 388J-1/2/3/4 night

and bad-weather fighters. The latter would have had Lichtenstein SN-2 radar in a pointed, 'solid' nose, a ventral pack with two 30 mm MK 108 and two 20 mm MG 151 cannon, and two upward-firing ('Schräge Musik') dorsal MG 151s; but, despite having the highest priority of all Ju 388 variants, no production was achieved. Only 10 Ju 388K-0 and five K-1 bombers (maximum load 3,000 kg; 6,614 lb) followed the V3 prototype, and these were not operational. Another uncompleted project was the Ju 388M-1, a four-seat torpedo carrier.

Junkers Ju 488 V403, with additional side view (**bottom**) of the **V401**

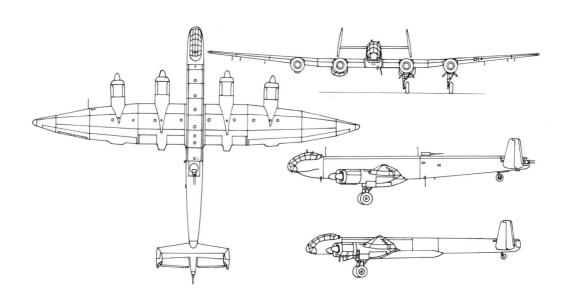

JUNKERS Ju 488

This 1944 strategic bomber was intended originally (Ju 488 V401 and V402) to utilise Ju 388K outer wings and pressurised forward fuselage, a Ju 188E rear fuselage, and a Ju 288C tail unit. It was later redesigned

(V403 to V406), retaining only the Ju 388K front fuselage, to have a 5,000 kg (11,023 lb) internal bomb load, increased fuel, and remotely-controlled barbettes in dorsal (two MG 151) and tail (two MG 131) positions. None, however, was completed. *Data: page 147.*

KLEMM
Kl 35

Formed in 1926, the Klemm company produced a varied range of lightplanes, of which one of the principal types was the tandem two-seat Kl 35, first flown in 1935. Two major production series were built: the Kl 35B (105 hp Hirth HM 504A-2), including a Kl 35BW twin-float variant, and the KL 35D. The former was exported to Czechoslovakia, Hungary, Lithuania, Romania and Sweden; the lower-powered Kl 35D, also available with float or ski gear, was produced primarily as a Luftwaffe basic trainer. In this capacity, and as a communications aircraft, it was used extensively from 1938–45. Thirty were supplied also to the wartime Slovakian Air Force. *Data : page 147.*

Klemm Kl 35 (RP + AG) tandem two-seat training aircraft

Aircraft type			Bf 108B		
Power plant			1 × 240 hp As 10C		
Accommodation			4		
Wing span	m	: ft in	10·612	: 34	9·8
Length overall	m	: ft in	8·291	: 27	2·4
Height overall	m	: ft in	2·30	: 7	6·6
Wing area	m²	: sq ft	16·40	: 176·53	
Weight empty	kg	: lb	880	: 1,940	
Weight loaded	kg	: lb	1,385	: 3,053	
Max wing loading	kg/m²	: lb/sq ft	84·45	: 17·29	
Max power loading	kg/hp	: lb/hp	5·77	: 12·72	
Max level speed	km/h	: mph	300	: 186	
at (height)	m	: ft	1,525	: 5,000	
Cruising speed	km/h	: mph	260	: 161	
at (height)	m	: ft	2,440	: 8,000	
Time to 3,000 m (9,845 ft)			16·8 min		
Service ceiling	m	: ft	6,000	: 19,685	
Range (max)	km	: miles	1,000	: 621	

MESSERSCHMITT
Bf 108

Almost 800 Bf 108s (first flight spring 1934) were built between 1934–44, including French wartime production, nearly all being of the Bf 108B Taifun (Typhoon) series for the Luftwaffe; post-war development by the SNCA du Nord added several hundred more. Luftwaffe duties included communications, liaison, pilot ferrying, target towing, rescue and supply; other operators included Bulgaria, Hungary, Japan, Romania, Switzerland, the USSR and Yugoslavia.

Messerschmitt Bf 108B (KG + EM) of an unidentified unit based in Cagliari, Sardinia, *ca* 1942. **Inset:** unit emblem of the same aircraft

Messerschmitt Bf 109F-4/Trop. of 3./JG 27, Ain-El Gazala, Libya, mid-June 1942 (aircraft of the Staffelkapitän, Oberleutnant Hans-Joachim Marseille)

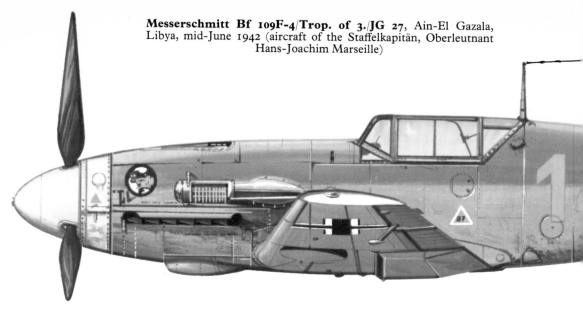

Messerschmitt Bf 109E-4/B of II./JG 54 'Grünherz', Eastern Front, 1942 (aircraft of the Geschwader Adjutant)

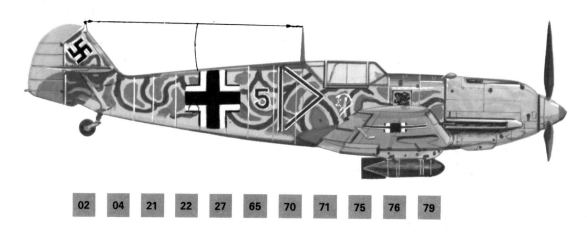

| 02 | 04 | 21 | 22 | 27 | 65 | 70 | 71 | 75 | 76 | 79 |

The **Bf 109E-4/B** fighter-bomber could carry one 250 kg or four 50 kg bombs on under-fuselage attachments

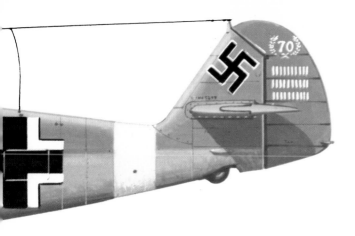

Top: Geschwader emblem of **JG 51**
'Mölders'; **above:** personal insignia
of Major Erich Hartmann

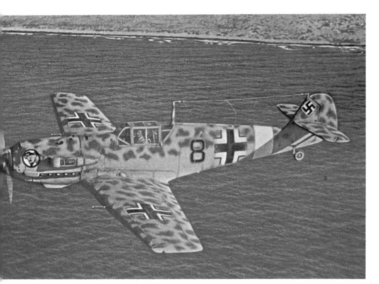

Messerschmitt Bf 109E-4/Trop. of I./JG 27, North Africa, summer
1941

**Messerschmitt Bf 109G-6/R6
Trop. of II./JG 53 'Pik-As'**, Italy,
1943–44

MESSERSCHMITT Bf 109

For 25 years the Bf 109 was in production somewhere in the world. It served the Luftwaffe for eight years, production during the years 1936–45 accounting for nearly two-thirds of Germany's entire output of single-seat fighters; and exported or licence-built versions equipped the air forces of nearly a dozen other nations. The total number built was well in excess of 33,000.

Designed by the Bayerische Flugzeug-werke AG in 1933 around Germany's most powerful aero-engine of the time, the 610 hp Junkers Jumo 210A, the Bf 109 V1 first prototype (D-IABI) actually made its first flight, in early September 1935, using a 695 hp Rolls-Royce Kestrel V. A Jumo 210A powered the V2, which flew in January 1936, followed by the intended prototype for the initial production series, the V3. First in-service fighter versions were the Bf 109B-1 and B-2, based on the V4 and V7 prototypes and armed with two 7·9 mm MG 17 machine-guns on top of the engine and a third MG 17 firing through the hollow propeller shaft. Deliveries of the B-1 (680 hp Jumo 210Da) began in April 1937 to JG 132, which was dispatched to join the Luftwaffe's Condor Legion fighting in the Spanish Civil War. On 11 November 1937 the Bf 109 V13 (D-IPKY), with a specially boosted DB 601 engine, set a new world absolute speed record of 610·55 km/h (379·38 mph). Despite its successful combat record in Spain, the Bf 109B's armament left room for improvement, and the number of MG 17s was increased to four in the C-1 (two over the engine and two in the wings) and five in the C-3 (by restoring the centre gun). The Bf 109Cs, which had 700 hp Jumo 210Ga engines, joined the Bs in Spain in 1938. In this year also, Arado, Erla, Fieseler, Focke-Wulf and WNF were brought into the Bf 109 production programme, and the BFW changed its name to Messerschmitt AG. Installation of the 986 hp DB 600Aa produced the Bf 109D series, with improved performance; small batches of Messerschmitt Bf 109Ds were also exported to Hungary and Switzerland.

At the outbreak of World War 2 the Luftwaffe had a strength of 1,056 Bf 109s. Many of these were Bf 109Ds, but this series was already being replaced in increasing numbers by the Bf 109E. This had first appeared (as the V14) in mid-1938, and the E-1 was produced both as a fighter (with four MG 17s) and as a fighter-bomber (carrying one 250 kg or four 50 kg bombs). Later E-1s standardised on 20 mm MG FF cannon in place of the two wing-mounted MG 17s. Against all types of opposing fighter throughout Poland, Czechoslovakia, France, Belgium, Holland and southern England, with the exception of the Spitfire (which it greatly outnumbered), the Bf 109E proved itself superior in both performance and manoeuvrability; only its range let it down. Production accelerated to the extent that Germany could afford to export substantial numbers of the Bf 109E-3 (which appeared at the end of 1939 and was the principal version to be used in the Battle of Britain) to Bulgaria, Hungary, Japan, Romania, Slovakia, Switzerland, the USSR and Yugoslavia. In addition, a small batch was built during 1941–43 by Dornier's Altenrhein factory in Switzerland. In July 1940 the Gerhard Fieseler-Werke began to convert 10 Bf 109E-1s to Bf 109T (for Träger: carrier) extended-span configuration. These were to have been development aircraft for the Bf 109T-1, intended for use aboard the proposed aircraft carrier *Graf Zeppelin*, but after the carrier programme was terminated the 60 T-1s ordered were completed instead as land-based T-2s. Various other E models, up to E-9, were produced for fighter and/or reconnaissance duties, with powerplant or equipment variations.

Meanwhile, Messerschmitt had been developing what was to become the finest of all the many versions, the Bf 109F. Powered by either a 1,200 hp DB 601N or a 1,350 hp DB 601E engine, the Bf 109F represented a considerable advance over earlier series in terms of both performance and cleanliness of line, and at last gave the Luftwaffe a fighter that could outmanoeuvre the Spitfire V. The entire fuselage was cleaner aerodynamically, culminating in a more rounded rudder, an unbraced tailplane and a retractable tail-wheel; the wings, of slightly increased span, were rounded off at the tips; and performance at all altitudes was better than that of earlier models. Production series ran from F-1 to F-6, with various sub-types. Several F-series aircraft were used as testbeds, the items evaluated including BMW 801 (radial) and Jumo 213 engines, a V-type tail unit, rocket weapons, and a nosewheel landing gear. A prototype never flown, but none the less of interest, was the Bf 109Z of 1943, in which two Bf 109Fs were 'twinned' by connecting them by a new, common wing centre-section and tailplane, the sole pilot being intended to occupy a cockpit in the port fuselage.

By 1942 the Bf 109F had been supplanted in production and service by the most numerous version, the Bf 109G. Heavier and less manoeuvrable than the Fs, with DB 605 engines and additional equipment, the 'Gustavs' were individually less successful; they were, however, used widely in Europe, the Middle East, and on the Eastern Front. Production showed no sign of decreasing; indeed, from a total of 2,628 Bf 109s accepted during 1941, German output increased to 2,664 in 1942, to 6,379 in 1943, and to 13,942 in 1944, despite the ever-wider dispersal of production centres to avoid the depredations of Allied bombers; and the figures for 1943 and 1944 were increased still further by Hungarian and Romanian licence production. More than 70 per cent of all Luftwaffe Bf 109s were G-series aircraft, covering a huge variety of models from G-1 to G-16 (with numerous sub-types), for fighter, fighter-bomber or reconnaissance duties. The G-6 in particular, equipped with

An early-production **Messerschmitt Bf 109E-1** fighter of **2./JG 20**, bearing the Staffel emblem later used also by 8./JG 51 'Mölders'. At the outbreak of war I./JG 20, based at Fürstenwalde, formed part of Luftflotte 1 in north-eastern Germany

This **Bf 109G-6** has on its cowling the emblem of **JG 53 'Pik-As'** (Ace of Spades). The G-6, which entered production in late 1942, was powered by a DB 605 engine, with boosted performance at altitude, and had a 30 mm MK 108 cannon mounted to fire through the propeller hub

Aircraft type			Bf 109E-3	Bf 109F-4	Bf 109G-6
Power plant			1 × 1,175 hp DB 601Aa	1 × 1,350 hp DB 601E-1	1 × 1,475 hp DB 605AM
Accommodation			1	1	1
Wing span	m	: ft in	9·87 : 32 4·6	9·924 : 32 6·7	9·924 : 32 6·7
Length overall	m	: ft in	8·64 : 28 4·2	8·848 : 29 0·3	8·848 : 29 0·3
Height overall	m	: ft in	3·20 : 10 6·0	3·20 : 10 6·0	3·20 : 10 6·0
Wing area	m²	: sq ft	16·40 : 176·53	16·20 : 174·38	16·20 : 174·38
Weight empty equipped	kg	: lb	2,125 : 4,685	2,390 : 5,269	2,675 : 5,897
Weight loaded	kg	: lb	2,665 : 5,875	2,900 : 6,393	3,150 : 6,944
Max wing loading	kg/m²	: lb/sq ft	162·50 : 33·28	179·01 : 36·66	194·44 : 39·82
Max power loading	kg/hp	: lb/hp	2·26 : 5·00	2·14 : 4·73	2·13 : 4·70
Max level speed	km/h	: mph	560 : 348	625 : 388	621 : 386
at (height)	m	: ft	4,440 : 14,565	6,500 : 21,325	6,900 : 22,640
Cruising speed	km/h	: mph	375 : 233	571 : 355	***500 : 311
at (height)	m	: ft	7,000 : 22,965	5,000 : 16,405	6,000 : 19,685
Time to height			5,000 m (16,405 ft) in 7·1 min	5,000 m (16,405 ft) in 5·2 min	5,000 m (16,405 ft) in approx 5·0 min
Service ceiling	m	: ft	10,500 : 34,450	12,000 : 39,375	11,550 : 37,895
Range	km	: miles	*660 : 410	**850 : 528	***1,000 : 621

* max, on internal fuel   ** with 300 litre drop-tank   *** approx

radar, was in widespread use as a night fighter from 1943. Recipients of export Bf 109Gs included Bulgaria, Finland, Hungary, Romania, Slovakia, Spain and Switzerland; and both Spain and Czechoslovakia continued licence production of various G models after the war.

The final wartime models to be used operationally by the Jagdgeschwadern were the Bf 109H and Bf 109K. Only a small number of the extended-span H-0 and H-1 were completed, as development priority for a high-altitude fighter was by then being given to the Focke-Wulf Ta 152. A few Bf 109Ks, basically refined versions of the Bf 109G with the 'Galland hood' of the later Gs, entered service in late 1944, but did not see much combat; and the prototype Bf 109L (Jumo 213E) did not lead to a production series.

MESSERSCHMITT Bf 110

The first twin-engined warplane to be designed by the Bayerische Flugzeugwerke, the Bf 110 was evolved originally to meet an early 1934 RLM specification for a Kampfzerstörer multi-purpose aircraft. This specification was later replaced by two separate ones, one of which resulted in the Ju 88. To meet the other, which in essence required a long-range penetration and escort fighter with heavy firepower, the Bf 110 was adopted. Three prototypes, all powered by 900 hp DB 600A engines, were ordered, and the first of these, the Bf 110 V1, made its first flight on 12 May 1936. Evaluated at Rechlin in early 1937, the Bf 110 had an excellent turn of speed—505 km/h (314 mph) had been recorded by the V1 on an early test flight—but it was heavy to fly and its manoeuvrability left something to be desired. Nevertheless, four pre-production Bf 110A-0s were built, each armed with four 7·9 mm MG 17 machine-guns in the nose and an MG 15 of similar calibre in the rear cockpit. Supplies of the DB 600 were still at a premium, causing the A-0s to be fitted instead with the 680 hp Jumo 210Da, but this was sadly inadequate for the job and performance suffered accordingly. The next

Bf 109K-4	Bf 109T-2	Bf 110C-1	Bf 110F-2	Bf 110G-4c/R3
1 × 2,000 hp DB 605ASCM	1 × 1,200 hp DB 601N	2 × 1,050 hp DB 601A-1	2 × 1,350 hp DB 601F	2 × 1,475 hp DB 605B-1
1	1	2 or 3	2	3
9·924 : 32 6·7	11·08 : 36 4·2	16·276 : 53 4·8	16·276 : 53 4·8	16·276 : 53 4·8
8·848 : 29 0·3	8·76 : 28 8·9	12·07 : 39 7·2	12·07 : 39 7·2	13·05 : 42 9·7
3·20 : 10 6·0	3·25 : 10 8·0	4·13 : 13 6·6	4·13 : 13 6·6	4·18 : 13 8·5
16·20 : 174·38	17·50 : 188·37	38·40 : 413·33	38·40 : 413·33	38·40 : 413·33
— : —	2,253 : 4,967	4,885 : 10,770	5,600 : 12,346	5,090 : 11,222
3,390 : 7,474	3,080 : 6,790	6,030 : 13,294	7,200 : 15,873	9,390 : 20,701
209·26 : 42·86	176·00 : 36·05	157·03 : 32·16	187·50 : 38·40	244·53 : 50·08
1·67 : 3·68	2·43 : 5·35	2·87 : 6·33	2·67 : 5·88	3·18 : 7·02
728 : 452	570 : 354	540 : 336	566 : 352	550 : 342
6,000 : 19,685	5,000 : 16,405	6,000 : 19,685	5,400 : 17,715	6,980 : 22,900
— : —	552 : 343	490 : 304	500 : 311	510 : 317
— : —	5,000 : 16,405	5,000 : 16,405	4,500 : 14,765	6,000 : 19,685
5,000 m (16,405 ft) in 3·0 min	5,000 m (16,405 ft) in approx 4·0 min	6,000 m (19,685 ft) in 10·2 min	6,000 m (19,685 ft) in 9·2 min	**** — : —
12,500 : 41,010	10,500 : 34,450	10,000 : 32,810	10,900 : 35,760	8,000 : 26,250
*575 : 357	**915 : 568	***1,095 : 680	***1,200 : 746	***900 : 559

* at 3,100 kg (6,834 lb) gross weight, max internal fuel   ** with 300 litre drop-tank   *** on internal fuel   **** S/L rate of climb 660 m (2,165 ft)/min

pre-production batch, of 10 Bf 110B-os, appeared in the spring of 1938 with 670 hp Jumo 210Ga engines, and these were used for the development of the B-1 initial production series, which also introduced a cleaner-shaped nose to which were added two 20 mm MG FF cannon. Unlike other leading Luftwaffe combat aircraft, the Bf 110 was not blooded in the Spanish Civil War, and most of the small number of B-1s built (about 40–50) were instead converted to B-2s or B-3s and allocated to a training role. The first series to enter operational service was thus the Bf 110C, which took advantage of the increased power of the 1,050 hp DB 601A-1 engine and introduced certain aerodynamic refinements including squared-off wingtips and a modified enclosure for the crew of two. The Bf 110C-1 began to enter service in April 1939, with I.(Z)/LG 1, and more than 300 Bf 110Cs had been delivered by the end of that year. Subtypes included the C-1 long-range fighter version; the similar C-2, with revised radio and electrics; the C-3, with improved MG FF/M cannon; the C-4, which introduced armour protection for the crew; the C-4/B

fighter-bomber, with four 250 kg bombs and 1,200 hp DB 601N engines; the reconnaissance C-5, with a camera replacing the MG FF guns; and, all with DB 601Ns, the C-5/N, C-6 and fighter-bomber C-7.

During the invasion of Poland, the Bf 110 was employed primarily for close support, and it was not until 1940, when it first encountered serious fighter opposition in the Battle of Britain, that its shortcomings as a fighter became evident, for no twin-engined design could have been expected to compete on equal terms with modern single-engined fighters. Inevitably, losses were such that the Bf 110s, originally assigned as escorts to the main bombing force, had themselves to be provided with an escort, of Bf 109s, for their own protection. After their withdrawal from the escort role, some early Cs were adapted for glider towing, notably with the Me 321. The D series were essentially longer-range counterparts to the Cs, the D-0 and D-1/R1 fighters having the unsuccessful 'Dackelbauch' (dachshund-belly) ventral auxiliary fuel tank and the D-1/R2, D-2 and D-3 a pair of underwing drop-tanks. The series also included, from September 1940, the

Two **Bf 110Fs** in all-black night fighter finish and bearing the markings of **7. Staffel, Nachtjagdgeschwader 4 (3C + GR and 3C + LR)**

Bf 110D-1/U1, the first true conversion for night fighting. However, by mid-1941 most C and D series aircraft had been transferred from European operations to the Mediterranean or Eastern Front, and production had begun to abate in anticipation of the Bf 110's replacement by the newer Me 210. Nevertheless, 1941 also saw the appearance of the Bf 110E series, in fighter and reconnaissance versions and, with up to 2,000 kg (4,409 lb) of ordnance, as a fighter-bomber. From early 1941 the early Bf 110F models (with the exception of the F-2, which had provision for two W Gr 21 rocket launchers under each wing) followed closely those of the E series except in powerplant, now changed again to

Although occasionally adopted by other units, the 'sharkmouth' decoration, shown on this **Bf 110C**, usually denoted an aircraft of **II. Gruppe of Zerstörergeschwader 76**, the 'Haifisch' (shark) Gruppe, which became operational on the Bf 110C-1 in spring/summer 1940. The concentration of forward-firing guns was formidable, but the Bf 110 was only lightly defended to the rear

Bf 110D long range Zerstörer with 'Dackelbauch' (dachshund-belly) ventral fuel tank, a feature soon discarded when its jettison mechanism proved to be unreliable

The **'Englandblitz'** insignia carried by most Nachtjagdgeschwader aircraft

21	22	23	24	71	76

Emblem of 1./NJG 3

Messerschmitt Bf 110G-4d/R3 (D5 + DS) of 8./NJG 3, 1944

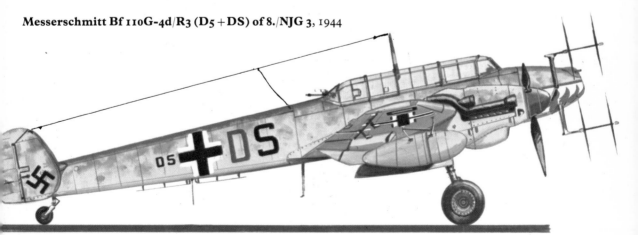

the 1,300 hp DB 601 F. The Bf 110F-4 of 1942 was the first purpose-built night fighter version, had a third crew member and, on some aircraft, two 30 mm MK 108 cannon in a ventral pack. First radar-equipped night fighter was the F-4a, with FuG 202 Lichtenstein BC. By the end of 1942, it was clear that the Me 210 was unlikely to be the 110's successor; production of the older type had therefore been increased and the DB 605-engined G series introduced. The G-1 to G-3 followed the pattern of earlier series, but the G-4 night fighter series emerged with many varied permutations of gun positions and calibres, including ventral packs, dorsal Schräge Musik installations, and heavy under-fuselage cannon. The G-4a, in service from autumn 1943, had Lichtenstein C-1 airborne interception radar; Lichtenstein SN-2 was added to this in the G-4b; and the C-1 radar deleted from the G-4c. Final series, produced alongside the Gs, was the Bf 110H. Somewhat unexpectedly, therefore, the Bf 110 reached its production peak in 1943 and 1944, with the last few dozen being delivered during the first two months of 1945 to make an overall total of about 6,050.

MESSERSCHMITT Bf 161 and Bf 162

Parallel developments of the Bf 110, neither of these aircraft entered production and comparatively few details of them are known. Two Bf 161s and three Bf 162s were built, the Bf 161 V1 two/three-seat high-speed reconnaissance aircraft (D-AABA) making its first flight in spring 1938 and the V2 about six months later. First flight of the Bf 162 V1 high-speed light bomber (D-AIXA) was made in the spring of 1937, followed by the V2 in September and the V3 in the following August. The Bf 162 had a combined internal/external bomb load of 1,000 kg (2,205 lb), and a single 7·9 mm MG 15 machine-gun in the rear cockpit. Performance of both types failed to improve noticeably upon that of the Bf 110, which continued in production, and the Bf 161 and Bf 162 prototypes were utilised instead for miscellaneous development duties, the Bf 162 V3, for example, being used to test the remotely-controlled gun barbettes designed for the Me 210. *Data : page 147.*

Messerschmitt Bf 161 V2 (CE + ??), a reconnaissance development of the Bf 110

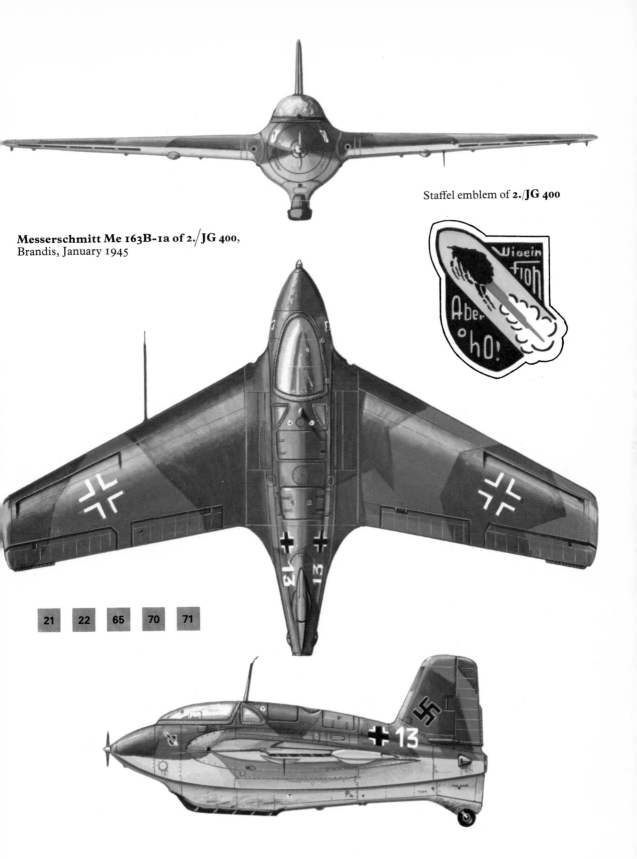

Messerschmitt Me 163B-1a of 2./JG 400,
Brandis, January 1945

Staffel emblem of **2./JG 400**

| 21 | 22 | 65 | 70 | 71 |

MESSERSCHMITT
Me 163 KOMET
(Comet)

Aircraft type		Me 163B-1A
Power plant		1 × 1,700 kg (3,748 lb) st HWK 509A-2
Accommodation		1
Wing span	m : ft in	9·33 : 30 7·3
Length overall	m : ft in	5·85 : 19 2·3
Height overall	m : ft in	2·76 : 9 0·7
Wing area	m² : sq ft	18·50 : 199·13
Weight empty	kg : lb	1,905 : 4,200
Weight loaded	kg : lb	4,310 : 9,502
Max wing loading	kg/m² : lb/sq ft	232·97 : 47·71
Max power loading	kg/kg st : lb/lb st	2·53 : 2·53
Max level speed	km/h : mph	960 : 596
above (height)	m : ft	3,000 : 9,845
S/L rate of climb	m/min : ft/min	4,875 : 15,995
Time to 12,100 m (39,700 ft)		3·35 min
Service ceiling	m : ft	12,100 : 39,700
Endurance after 796 km/h (495 mph) climb		2·50 min
Max powered endurance		7·50 min

Although it arrived too late and in numbers too few to affect the outcome of World War 2, the Komet was quite successful during the nine months or so that it was in action, thanks mainly to its speed, its unconventional armament, and an element of surprise. Probably the most radical combat aircraft of the entire conflict, it was based upon the experimental DFS 194, designed in 1938 by Prof Alexander M. Lippisch and later transferred to Messerschmitt for further development. But for differences between Lippisch and Prof Willy Messerschmitt, coupled with delays in deliveries of its rocket engines, it would almost certainly have been available much earlier. The first two prototypes were flown unpowered in the spring of 1941, the Me 163 V1 being transferred to Peenemünde later that year to receive its 750 kg (1,653 lb) st HWK R.II rocket motor. The first rocket-powered flight was made in August 1941, and in trials the Komet soon exhibited speeds of more than 1,000 km/h (621 mph). Ten unpowered Me 163As were built in late 1941 as conversion trainers. The airframe of the Me 163 V3, on which were based the 70 Me 163B-0 and B-1 production

interceptors ordered, was completed in May 1942, but more than a year then elapsed before its HWK 509A engine became available. By then nearly 40 production aircraft were also complete and awaiting powerplants. Additional Komet production was undertaken by Klemm, the overall total being slightly more than 350. The first Luftwaffe unit to receive the Me 163, JG 400, made its operational debut on 16 August 1944 against US Eighth Air Force B-17s over Germany. Armament comprised a 30mm MK 108 cannon in each wing root and either four 50mm R4M rockets in each wing (firing vertically upward) or 12 conventionally-firing rockets beneath each wing. However, the definitive version was nearly a ton heavier than its original designed weight, necessitating auxiliary booster rockets for take-off, while landings were hazardous in the extreme. All too often the Me 163, landing on its keel/skid with highly inflammable fuel still in its tanks, would come literally to a comet-like end, with fatal results for its pilot. By 1945 the pressurised Me 163C (HWK 509C motor) had reached the pre-production stage, and a prototype had also been flown of a derivative known as the Me 163D. Development was transferred to Junkers, which built a second prototype, known as the Ju 248 V1, with pressurised cockpit and retractable tricycle landing gear. This first flew under power in September 1944, but intended production (as the Me 263A-1) was never achieved.

MESSERSCHMITT Me 210 and Me 410 HORNISSE (Hornet)

The Me 210 was intended to be a successor to the Zerstörer Bf 110; instead, it proved to be an abysmal failure. RLM approval of the design in mid-1938 was accompanied by an option for 1,000 production aircraft, but right from the first flight on 5 September 1939 by the twin-finned Me 210 V1 (D-AABF) its troubles began. This aircraft showed marked instability in flight, and attempts to remedy this resulted in a large-area single fin and rudder being substituted on the V1 and subsequent prototypes. Two initial production models were ordered: the Me 210A-1 Zerstörer and A-2 dive-bomber, both with DB 601F engines. The A-1 was armed with two 20 mm MG 151 cannon and two 7·9 mm MG 17 machine-guns grouped in the nose, plus a 13 mm MG 131 rearward-firing gun in a remotely-controlled, electrically-operated barbette on each side of the mid-fuselage. The A-2, in addition, had an internal bay for up to 1,000 kg (2,205 lb) of bombs. However, despite the use through 1940–41 for development and service trials of no fewer than 16 prototypes, eight of the 94 pre-production Me 210A-0s, and 13 production A-1s, by no means all of the Me 210's undesirable handling qualities had been eradicated before, in early 1942, all production was stopped and that of the Bf 110 was increased. It was later resumed for a brief period, but the final total completed in Germany was only 352, plus 267 C-series aircraft built under licence in Hungary (of which 108 were supplied to the Luftwaffe). Designated Me 210Ca-1 (Zerstörer/dive-bomber) and Me 210C-1 (reconnaissance/Zerstörer), these were generally similar to the A series but with DB 605B engines and improved handling characteristics resulting from the introduction of a redesigned, deeper rear fuselage and automatic leading-edge slots on the outer wings. These modifications were then applied retrospectively to some existing Me 210A-1s, which in August 1942 became operational with 16./KG 6 in Holland and later with III./ZG 1 in Sicily and other units in the Mediterranean area.

In the search for an Me 210 replacement, the RLM by-passed the extended-span, pressurised Me 310 (whose prototype, the Me 210 V17, flew on 11 September 1943) in favour of the more straightforward Me 410 Hornisse. This embodied the important wing and fuselage improvements of the later 210s (several of which acted as Me 410 development aircraft) and, with a change to DB 603A engines, the Me 410 V1 flew for the first time in the autumn of 1942. In the following January the Luftwaffe accepted its first

02 21 22 25 70 74 75 76

Gruppe emblem of **III./ZG 1** (later redesignated **II./ZG 26**)

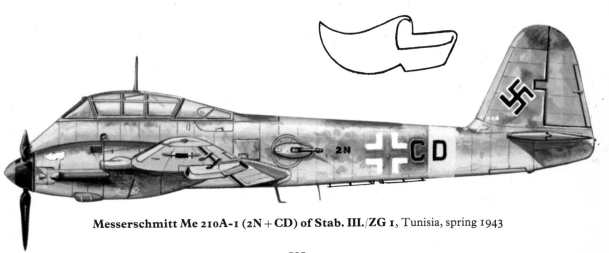

Messerschmitt Me 210A-1 (2N + CD) of Stab. III./ZG 1, Tunisia, spring 1943

Aircraft type		Me 210A-1	Me 410A-1/U2
Power plant		2 × 1,350 hp DB 601F	2 × 1,750 hp DB 603A
Accommodation		2	2
Wing span	m : ft in	16·34 : 53 7·3	16·358 : 53 8·0
Length overall	m : ft in	12·12 : 39 9·2	12·56 : 41 2·5
Height overall	m : ft in	4·28 : 14 0·5	5·207 : 17 1·0
Wing area	m² : sq ft	36·20 : 389·65	36·20 : 389·65
Weight empty equipped	kg : lb	7,070 : 15,586	7,518 : 16,574
Weight loaded (max)	kg : lb	9,705 : 21,396	9,650 : 21,275
Max wing loading	kg/m² : lb/sq ft	268·09 : 54·91	266·57 : 54·60
Max power loading	kg/hp : lb/hp	3·59 : 7·92	2·75 : 6·07
Max level speed	km/h : mph	563 : 350	625 : 388
at (height)	m : ft	5,430 : 17,815	6,700 : 21,980
Time to 6,000 m (19,685 ft)		12·4 min	10·7 min
Service ceiling	m : ft	8,900 : 29,200	10,000 : 32,810
Range (max)	km : miles	1,820 : 1,130	1,690 : 1,050

02

21

22

70

74

75

76

Me 410A-1s; units of KG 2 were operational with the Hornisse by spring 1943; and by 1944 a total of 1,160 Me 410s (plus some Me 210 conversions) had been manufactured. Several A and B sub-types were produced, with variations in armament and equipment, for service as 'heavy' fighters, bomber destroyers and photo-reconnaissance aircraft. Typical armament of the Me 410A-1 was similar to that already listed for the Me 210A-1, but other variations included the addition of two more MG 151s in the bombbay (U2 versions of the Me 410A-1, B-1 and B-2); a single 50mm BK 5 cannon (Me 410A-

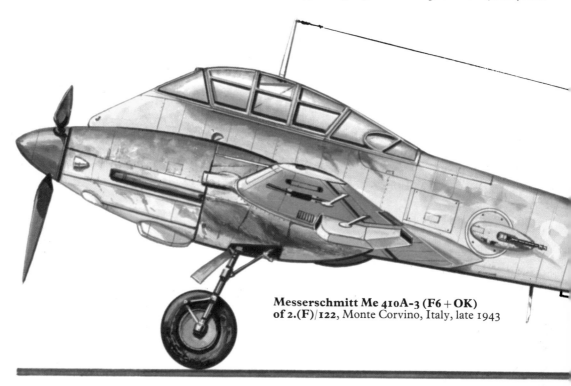

Messerschmitt Me 410A-3 (F6 + OK)
of 2.(F)/122, Monte Corvino, Italy, late 1943

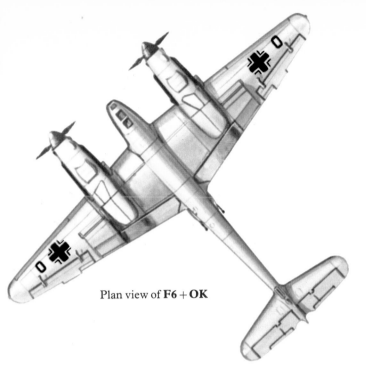

Plan view of **F6 + OK**

1/U4); or two MG 151s, two MG 17s and a BK 5 (Me 410A-2/U4). Some models had a ventral pack with two more MG 151s; others had two 30 mm MK 103 or MK 108 cannon in the bombbay. The Me 410A-2/U2 night fighter, which served with NJG 1 and 5, was equipped with two MK 108s, two MG 151s and Lichtenstein SN-2 radar. The 210 mm W Gr 21 rocket projectile became an effective weapon on some Me 410Bs, a rotary launcher in the bomb-bay being able to quick-fire six of these weapons in single shots. The Me 410A-3 and B-3 had the MG 17 guns deleted and bomb-bay fairings containing three aerial cameras. The Me 410B-5 carried one or two torpedos under the fuselage, and the B-6 also was employed in an anti-shipping role. The proposed B-7 and B-8 were for day and night reconnaissance, but did not enter service; the projected Me 410D (wooden outer wings) and high-altitude Me 410C and H (extended-span wings) failed to materialise.

Messerschmitt Me 410A-3 (F6 + WK) of 2.(F)/122

Staffel emblem of **2.(F)/122**

Messerschmitt Me 261 V2 (BJ + CQ) prototype very long range aircraft

MESSERSCHMITT Me 261

After staging the 1936 Olympic Games, Germany approved in 1937 the development of this ultra-long-range aircraft, one of whose projected tasks was to fly the Olympic torch non-stop to Tokyo in 1940. Also to be used for distance record attempts, it was known unofficially as the 'Adolfine' because of Hitler's personal support. Three prototypes were started in spring 1939, all having a slender fuselage almost swallowed by the extremely thick wings. Powerplant was a pair of DB606A/B (coupled DB601) engines in the V1 and V2, or more powerful DB610A/Bs (coupled DB605) in the V3, the wings forming a huge integral fuel tank; the landing gear was fully retractable. Development, halted in August 1939, was resumed in mid-1940, first flights taking place on 23 December 1940 (V1), and in spring 1942 (V2) and early 1943 (V3). The five-seat V1 and V2 were scrapped after being seriously damaged during an Allied air attack in 1944. The V3, which carried a seven-man crew, gave an indication of its capabilities on 16 April 1943 with a 10-hour flight covering 4,500 km (2,796 miles), and from mid-1943 was used for extra-long-range reconnaissance by the Aufklärungsgruppe ob d L. *Data: page 147.*

MESSERSCHMITT Me 262

Design of the Me 262 jet fighter, which had the Messerschmitt Projekt number 1065, began about a year before the outbreak of World War 2. But, due to delays in the development and delivery of satisfactory engines, the depredations caused by Allied air attacks, a troublesome development programme, and Hitler's refusal to be advised regarding its most appropriate role, it was six years before the aircraft entered Luftwaffe squadron service. A mockup of the aircraft was completed during the latter half of 1939, examination of which prompted the RLM to order three flying prototypes in the spring of 1940. These were all completed by early 1941, long before the arrival of their engines; so, to test the basic attributes of the airframe, the Me 262 V1 (PC + UA) made its first flight on 18 April 1941 with dummy jet-engine nacelles under the wings and a single 700 hp Jumo 210G piston engine mounted in the nose. On 25 March 1942 it made a barely-successful attempt to fly with two underwing BMW 003 jet engines, but still with the nose-mounted Jumo 210G. The first all-jet flight was made on 18 July 1942, when the Me 262 V3 (PC + UC) took off under the power of two 840 kg (1,852 lb) st Jumo 004A turbojets. Many more prototypes were completed and used for trials with various armament and equipment installations, and from the V5 onward (first flight 26 June 1943) a tricycle landing gear was substituted for the original tailwheel type. Plans for priority mass-production were seriously affected by Allied air attacks upon Messerschmitt's Regensburg factory, and there were numerous development problems involving engine fires and failures, landing gear collapses, guns jamming, and in-flight break-ups. Engine deliveries began in earnest in June 1944, permitting deliveries of production Me 262As to begin, and 513 had been accepted by the Luftwaffe by the end of the year—less than 40 per cent of the planned number. The Me 262's flying qualities were excellent, and a pre-series batch of 23 A-os was accepted in the spring of 1944. These were allocated to the Erprobrungs-stelle at Rechlin and the conversion unit EKdo 262, the latter unit becoming, on 25 July 1944, the first to fire the Me 262's guns in anger. The two principal basic production versions to become operational were the Me 262A-1a Schwalbe (swallow) inter-ceptor and the Me 262A-2a Sturmvogel (stormbird) fighter-bomber. The former was built in numerous sub-types with four 30 mm MK 108 cannon in the nose, or alternative armament installations; the latter, produced as a result of Hitler's insistence upon developing the aircraft as a bomber, had external racks for one 1,000 kg or two 500 kg bombs. Other variants included the A-1a/V 083, with a single 50 mm BK 5 cannon in the nose; the A-1b, with twelve 55 mm R4M unguided rocket projectiles under each wing; the one-off A-2a/U2 with a glazed nose-cap over a prone bomb-aiming position; the ground attack Me 262A-3a; and the photo-reconnaissance Me 262A-1a/U3 and Me 262A-5a. A tandem two-seat trainer version was designated Me 262B-1a, and one prototype was completed of a proposed two-seat night fighter, the Me 262B-2a. This incorporated a longer fuselage, containing more fuel, and a Schräge Musik installation of two MK 108 cannon aft of the cockpit, firing upward. The B-2a did not enter production, but several B-1as were converted for night fighting (without the extended fuselage) and redesignated Me 262B-1a/U1. These were employed quite successfully by the Kommando

Me 262A-2a of 1./KG 51

Two-seat Me 262B-1a

Aircraft type		*Me 262A-2a
Power plant		2 × 900 kg (1,984 lb) st Jumo 004B series Orkan
Accommodation		1
Wing span	m : ft in	12·48 : 40 11·5
Length overall	m : ft in	10·605 : 34 9·5
Height overall	m : ft in	3·83 : 12 6·8
Wing area	m² : sq ft	21·68 : 233.36
Weight empty equipped	kg : lb	4,420 : 9,744
Weight loaded	kg : lb	6,396 : 14,101
Max wing loading	kg/m² : lb/sq ft	295·02 : 60·42
Max power loading	kg/kg st : lb/lb st	3·55 : 3·55
Max level speed	km/h : mph	870 : 540
at (height)	m : ft	6,000 : 19,685
Time to 9,000 m (29,530 ft)		13·1 min
Service ceiling	m : ft	11,450 : 37,565
Range (internal fuel)	km : miles	1,050 : 652

* weights and performance for A-1a; A-2a generally similar

21 22 70 74 76

Messerschmitt Me 262A-2a of 1./KG 51, Achmer, spring 1945 (see
photograph on previous page)

Geschwader emblem of
KG 51 'Edelweiss'

Welter, or 10./NJG 11 as it was later known. The few Me 262C models completed before VE-day were fitted with various rocket motors in the fuselage to boost the fighter's climb rate. Although little more than 500 Me 262s had been produced by December 1944, by the end of the war the total had risen to about 1,430. Probably less than a quarter of these saw front-line service, and losses among them were quite heavy, even though relatively few losses were realised in combat. Despite this, their destruction of Allied bombers and fighters was greater than one for one, and JV 44, the top-scoring Me 262 interceptor unit, achieved some 50 'kills' in little more than a month's operations in 1945. In air-to-air combat the Me 262 never engaged its British counterpart, the twin-jet Gloster Meteor (which was slower and less well armed); conversely, many Me 262s were destroyed by Allied Mustang, Spitfire, Tempest and Thunderbolt piston-engined fighters.

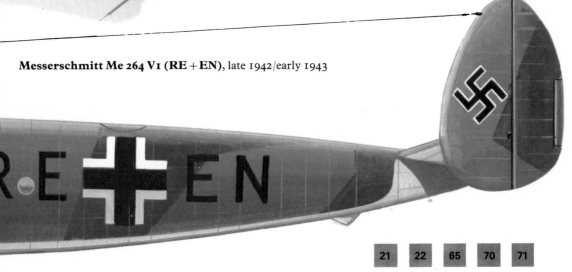

Messerschmitt Me 264 VI (RE + EN), late 1942/early 1943

| 21 | 22 | 65 | 70 | 71 |

MESSERSCHMITT Me 264

Aircraft type			*Me 264 V3		
Power plant			4 × 1,700 hp BMW 801 D or G		
Accommodation			6		
Wing span	m	: ft in	43·00	: 141	0·9
Length overall	m	: ft in	21·33	: 69	11·8
Height overall	m	: ft in	4·28	: 14	0·5
Wing area	m²	: sq ft	127·70	: 1,374·55	
Weight empty equipped	kg	: lb	21,150	: 46,627	
Weight loaded	kg	: lb	45,540	: 100,398	
Max wing loading	kg/m²	: lb/sq ft	356·61	: 73·04	
Max power loading	kg/hp	: lb/hp	6·69	: 14·76	
Max level speed	km/h	: mph	545	: 338	
at (height)	m	: ft	6,100	: 20,015	
Cruising speed	km/h	: mph	350	: 217	
at (height)	m	: ft	8,000	: 26,245	
S/L rate of climb	m/min	: ft/min	120	: 393	
Service ceiling	m	: ft	8,000	: 26,245	
Range (max)	km	: miles	15,000	: 9,320	

* weights and performance estimated

Known unofficially as the 'Amerika-Bomber', the Me 264 was designed as an un-armed, extra-long-range bomber with a 45-hour endurance, intended to be able to carry 1,800 kg (3,968 lb) of bombs from Berlin to New York. Work on three proto-types started in 1941, the Me 264 V1 (RE + EN) flying for the first time in December 1942, powered by four Jumo 211J-1 engines in standard Ju 88A-4 nacelles and carrying 25,250 litres (5,554 Imp gallons) of fuel in the wings. When, after the USA entered the war, the Amerika-Bomber concept was revised to a six-engined aircraft with a greater bomb load, development of the V2 and V3 was continued in-stead for the reconnaissance role (Me 264A), with extended-span wings, BMW 801 engines, and flares, three cameras and extra fuel tankage in the bomb bay. Engines and vital parts of the airframe were armoured, and a defensive armament of two 20 mm MG 151 and four 13 mm MG 131 guns was planned. But the V2 was des-troyed by Allied air attack in late 1943, before it had flown, and with the V1 allocated to Transportstaffel 5, only the V3 remained. So far as is known this was not completed, and the entire Me 264 programme was abandoned at the end of 1944. A number of further versions were projected, including some with turboprop or auxiliary turbojet engines; and one towing an Me 328 escort fighter.

Me 264 V1 long range bomber

MESSERSCHMITT Me 309

Although not considered of high priority, work on a successor to the Bf 109 was started in late 1940. Obvious targets for improve-ment were speed, armament and—in the light of Battle of Britain experience—operational radius. The Me 309, of which nine proto-types were ordered initially, emerged featur-ing a retractable tricycle landing gear, thin-section wings, a retractable ventral radiator,

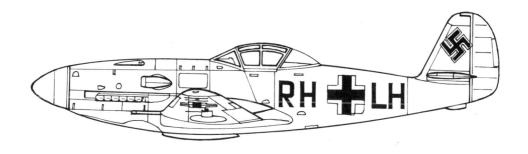

Messerschmitt Me 309 V4 (RH + LH) experimental single-seat fighter, an unsuccessful attempt to produce an improved development of the ubiquitous Bf 109

and a pressurised cockpit with a bubble canopy. The Me 309 V1 (GE + CU), with a DB 603A-1 engine, first flew on 18 July 1942. Early trials revealed the need for modifications to the tail configuration, engine cowling and undercarriage retraction system, but even after these, the handling and stability left much to be desired, and the new fighter could still be out-turned by the Bf 109G. The prototype order was cut to four, of which the V2 suffered irreparable damage when landing after its first flight on 29 November 1942. The V3 and V4, with DB 605B engines (later fitted also to the V1),

appeared in March and July 1943, but by then the programme had been virtually shelved. The V4, destroyed later by Allied air attack, carried the armament intended for the production Me 309A-2 'heavy' fighter, comprising two 13 mm MG 131 machine-guns in the upper engine decking, two 20 mm MG 151 cannon and two MG 131s in the wing roots, and two 30 mm MK 108 cannon in the outer wings. The Me 309A-1 'light' version was to have had two MG 131s and a single MK 108 only, the B-1 being similarly armed but capable also of carrying two 250 kg bombs. *Data : page 147.*

MESSERSCHMITT Me 321 and Me 323 GIGANT (Giant)

The huge Me 321 Gigant transport glider, hurriedly designed in the autumn of 1940, flew for the first time on 25 February 1941 and was in service in large numbers less than four months later. It could accommodate up to 200 troops, or some 22 tonnes of cargo or military equipment, and served principally on the Eastern Front; two versions (100 of each) were built as the Me 321A-1 and B-1. The initial aero-tow method of launch using

Me 321 Gigant in its static unladen attitude, with nosewheels off the ground

a trio of Bf 110s, usually with rocket assistance, proved unsatisfactory; later, the use of a single Ju 290A-1 or 'twin' He 111Z proved more practical. In 1941, Ing Degel of Messerschmitt undertook the development of a self-powered version, the Me 323, avoiding encroachment upon domestic engine production by utilising captured French Gnome-Rhône 14N radial engines. Two prototypes were converted from Me 321s, the four-engined Me 323 V1 (prototype for the Me 323C) making its first flight in spring 1942. However, it was quickly apparent that four engines were insufficient, and all effort was concentrated on the Me 323D prototype, the six-engined V2. The Me 323D followed the Me 321 into production, a pre-series batch of 10 D-os being delivered from August 1942, followed a month later by

Aircraft type			Me 323E-2		
Power plant			6 × 1,140 hp Gnome-Rhône 14N 48/49		
Accommodation			11 + 130		
Wing span	m	: ft in	55·00	: 180	5·4
Length overall	m	: ft in	28·50	: 93	6·0
Height overall	m	: ft in	9·60	: 31	6·0
Wing area	m²	: sq ft	300·00	: 3,229·17	
Weight empty equipped	kg	: lb	29,600	: 65,256	
Weight loaded	kg	: lb	45,000	: 99,208	
Max wing loading	kg/m²	: lb/sq ft	150·00	: 30·72	
Max power loading	kg/hp	: lb/hp	6·57	: 14·50	
Max level speed	km/h	: mph	285	: 177	
at (height)	m	: ft	S/L		
Cruising speed	km/h	: mph	250	: 155	
at (height)	m	: ft	S/L		
S/L rate of climb	m/min	: ft/min	120	: 394	
Service ceiling	m	: ft	4,500	: 14,765	
Range	km	: miles	*1,300	: 808	

*at 4,000 m (13,125 ft)

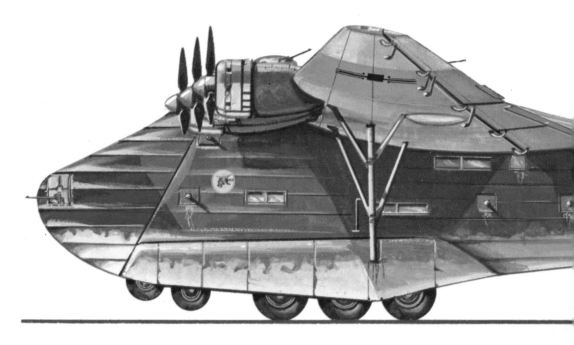

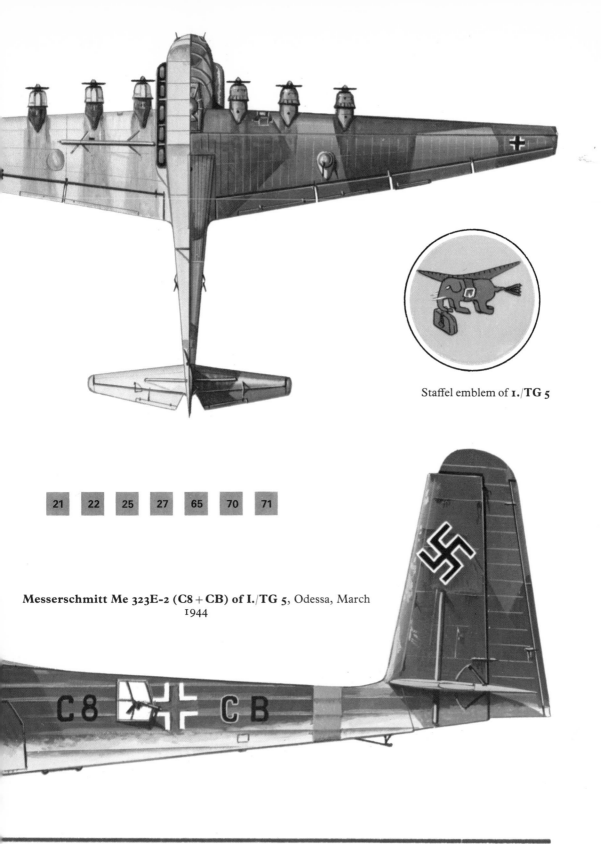

Staffel emblem of **I./TG 5**

21 22 25 27 65 70 71

Messerschmitt Me 323E-2 (C8 + CB) of I./TG 5, Odessa, March
1944

the D-1 initial production model, with accommodation for 120 troops, 60 stretcher cases or equivalent cargo. (The D-2, differing only in having two-blade wooden, instead of three-blade metal propellers, was less satisfactory.) The D-1's four 7·9mm MG15 machine-guns were replaced by five 13mm MG131s in the chief production model, the Me323D-6; however, additional weapons were often carried, and the experimental Me323E-2/WT mounted no fewer than 11 cannon and four machine-guns. The E-1 and E-2 series, based on the V13 prototype, had strengthened airframes, carried more fuel, and in the E-2 introduced, between the centre and outer engines on each wing, a 20mm MG151 cannon in a power-operated turret. The V14 and V16 were powered respectively by Jumo 211F and 211R engines, the latter being a prototype for the proposed Me323F series, but no Jumo-engined version was after all produced. Overall Me323 production, by Messerschmitt and Zeppelin factories,

Me 323D-6 disgorging an army truck

amounted to 198, excluding prototypes. The Me323 was an invaluable supply transport on the Eastern Front, but in North Africa and elsewhere its slow speed and difficult handling made it vulnerable, despite being well-armed and battleworthy. After heavy losses in the evacuation of Tunisia, little more was heard of it.

MESSERSCHMITT Me 328

Based upon earlier studies by DFS and Messerschmitt, the Me328 gathered momentum in spring 1943. Intended initially as a cheap, semi-expendable parasite fighter to accompany the He177 or Me264 bombers, it was proposed in three fighter and three fighter-bomber versions: the short-span Me328A-1, with two MG151 guns and two pulse-jet engines; the longer-span A-2, with four pulse-jets and four guns (two MK103s being added); the similar A-3, able to refuel in flight; the B-1 and B-2, similar to the A-1/A-2 but carrying a 1,000kg bomb; and the B-3, with a 1,400kg bomb. Three prototypes were built by DFS, and seven by Jacob Schweyer Segelflugzeugbau, and the V1 was first air-tested, unpowered, above a Do217E carrier aircraft. However, the design was aerodynamically poor; the Argus As014 pulse-jets were tried in twos and fours, beneath the wings and on the fuselage sides,

but their noise and vibration caused constant problems; and the Me328A series was eventually abandoned. Schweyer began to build some Me328B-0s, which it was proposed might be used by 5./KG200 as glider-bombs, but these were never completed, and the projected Me328C, with a Jumo 004B turbojet replacing the pulse-jets, did not materialise. *Data: page 147.*

A DFS-built prototype of the **Me 328**

MESSERSCHMITT P.1101

Design of Messerschmitt's Projekt 1101, initially for swept-wing research, began in mid-1942; but when, in autumn 1944, the RLM called for a single-jet fighter faster than the Me 262, it was one of eight designs submitted by Blohm und Voss, Focke-Wulf, Heinkel, Junkers and Messerschmitt. With swept-back wings and tail married to a pod-and-boom fuselage, the P.1101 had an ejection seat, retractable tricycle landing gear, 1,760 litres (387 Imp gallons) of fuel, and a proposed armament of two or four 30 mm MK 108 cannon. The intended Heinkel-Hirth turbojet of 1,300 kg (2,866 lb) st being unavailable, a 900 kg (1,984 lb) st Jumo 004B was selected instead; but the P.1101 was halted by the RLM at the end of 1944. Messerschmitt continued with its development privately, with the first flight scheduled for June 1945, and planned to use it for flight-testing pre-fixed wing sweep angles of 35, 40 and 45 degrees. However, at the end of April the prototype was captured by advancing US forces when little more than 80 per cent complete. Later shipped to the United States, it was stored at Wright Field until 1948, when Bell Aircraft Corporation used some of its features in the Bell X-5 variable-geometry research aircraft; but the P.1101 itself never flew. *Data: page 147*.

Uncompleted prototype of the **Messerschmitt P.1101**

SIEBEL Si 204

The Si 204A, first flown on 23 May 1941, was developed for DLH from the pre-war Flugzeugbau Halle (originally Klemm) Fh 104A Hallore five-seat light transport. Essentially, the Si 204A was a scaled-up, twin-tailed derivative of the Fh 104A, powered by two 360hp Argus As 410A engines and seating eight passengers plus a crew of two; most of those built were taken over by the Luftwaffe as light transports or liaison aircraft. The more powerful Si 204D was chosen by the Luftwaffe to succeed the Fw 58 as the standard blind-flying, navigation and radio trainer for the Flugzeug-führerschulen, and could accommodate five trainees plus a two-man crew. Chief external difference from the Si 204A was the replacement of the latter's 'solid' nose and stepped flight deck windows by a fully-glazed and unstepped forward fuselage. The Si 204D was normally unarmed, and remained in Luftwaffe service throughout World War 2, latterly also for radar training, in addition to such other duties as VIP or freight transport, communications and casualty evacuation. Some Si 204Ds were equipped with a 7.9 mm machine-gun in a dorsal turret, and were fitted with racks for small bombs and/or rocket projectile launchers beneath the fuselage and wings; this version was employed by at least one Nachtschlachtstaffel on the Eastern Front, in late 1944, for night ground attack. Most of the 1,175 Si 204A/Ds built during the war were produced in German-held factories in Czechoslovakia (Aero and BMM) and France (SNCA du Centre). After the war, SNCAC built about 350 more, in slightly modified form with Renault engines, as NC 701 (military Si 204D) and NC 702 (civil Si 204A) Martinets; Aero also built a number postwar as C-3 or C-103 military and civil transports.

Siebel Si 204D-1 of
Flugzeugführerschule (B)
18, Neu Biberg, June 1945

| 21 |
| 22 |
| 65 |
| 70 |
| 71 |

Emblem of **FFS (B) 18**

Aircraft type		Si 204D-1
Power plant		2 × 600 hp As 411
Accommodation		2 + 5
Wing span	m : ft in	21·28 : 69 9·8
Length overall	m : ft in	11·95 : 39 2·5
Height overall	m : ft in	4·40 : 14 5·2
Wing area	m² : sq ft	46·00 : 495·14
Weight empty	kg : lb	3,950 : 8,708
Weight loaded	kg : lb	5,600 : 12,346
Max wing loading	kg/m² : lb/sq ft	121·74 : 24·93
Max power loading	kg/hp : lb/hp	4·66 : 10·28
Max level speed	km/h : mph	364 : 226
at (height)	m : ft	3,000 : 9,845
Cruising speed	km/h : mph	340 : 211
at (height)	m : ft	3,000 : 9,845
Time to 1,000 m (3,280 ft)		3·3 min
Service ceiling	m : ft	7,500 : 24,600
Range	km : miles	1,600 : 994

PRINCIPAL GERMAN CENTRES OF AIRCRAFT AND AERO-ENGINE PRODUCTION

(supplemented by other factories in Austria, Czechoslovakia, France, Hungary, Poland, Switzerland et al)

46 Lübeck (Do, Fw)
47 Lübz (He)
48 Magdeburg (Ju)
49 Marienburg (Fw)
50 Melsungen (Hs)
51 Merseburg (Ju)
52 München (BMW, Do)
53 Neubrandenburg (Ar, Fw)
54 Nordhausen (Fi/Mittelwerke)
55 Oberammergau (Me)
56 Oberpfaffenhofen (Do, Me)
57 Oldenburg (Fa)
58 Ölsnitz (He)
59 Oschersleben (AGO)
60 Rathenow (Ar)
61 Regensburg (Me)
62 Reinickendorf (Do, He)
63 Remsfeld (Hs)
64 Rostock (He)
65 Rövershagen (He)
66 Schönebeck (Fi/VW)
67 Schwäbisch Hau (Me)
68 Schwerin (Fw)
69 Sonneberg (Go)
70 Stassfurt (He)
71 Sternberg (Do)
72 Stuttgart (DB, Hirth/He)
73 Waldeck (Hs)
74 Waldsee (Ba)
75 Warnemünde (Ar, Fw)
76 Wega (Hs)
77 Wenzendorf (BV, Me)
78 Wernigerode (Bü)
79 Wismar (Do, Fw)
80 Wittenberge (Ar)

1 Adorf (He)
2 Ainring (DFS)
3 Allmansweiler (Do)
4 Anklam (Ar, Fw)
5 Aschersleben (Ju)
6 Augsburg (Me)
7 Babelsberg (Ar)
8 Bad Tölz (Fl)
9 Barth (He)
10 Berlin (As, Berlin, Bü, Do, Fl, Fw, He, Hs)
11 Bernburg (Ju)
12 Böblingen (Kl)
13 Bonn (Ho)
14 Brandenburg (Ar, Bramo)

15 Braunschweig (MIAG)
16 Bremen (Fw)
17 Breslau (Ju)
18 Cottbus (Fw)
19 Darmstadt (DFS)
20 Dessau (Ju)
21 Dingolfing (Me)
22 Erfurt (Fw)
23 Fallersleben (Fi/VW)
24 Friedrichroda (Go)
25 Friedrichshafen (Do, Ze)
26 Fritzlar (Ju)
27 Fürth (Go)
28 Gändersheim (He)

29 Giebelstadt (Me)
30 Gotha (Go)
31 Halberstadt (Fw, Ju)
32 Halle (Si)
33 Hamburg (BV)
34 Hannover (Fw)
35 Hersfeld (Hs)
36 Hoyenkamp (Fa)
37 Kassel (Fi, Hs)
38 Köthen (Ju)
39 Krakow (He)
40 Laupheim (Fa)
41 Lechfeld (Me)
42 Leipheim (Me)
43 Leipzig (Erla, Ju)
44 Leopoldshall (Ju)
45 Lindau (Do)

TECHNICAL DATA (MINOR TYPES)

Aircraft type	Power plant	Seats	Wing span (m / ft in)	Length (m / ft in)	Wing area (m² / sq ft)	Weight loaded (kg / lb)	Max speed (km/h / mph)	at (height) (m / ft)	Service ceiling (m / ft)	Range (km / miles)	Remarks
Ar 66C	1 × 240 hp As 10C	2	10·00 / 32 9·7	8·30 / 27 2·8	29·63 / 318·93	1,330 / 2,932	210 / 130	S/L	4,500 / 14,765	715 / 444	
Ar 68E-1	1 × 680 hp Jumo 210Ea	1	11·00 / 36 1·1	9·50 / 31 2·0	27·30 / 293·85	2,020 / 4,453	335 / 208	2,650 / 8,695	8,100 / 26,575	500 / 310	
Ar 95A-1	1 × 880 hp BMW 132Dc	2	12·50 / 41 0·1	11·00 / 36 5·0	45·38 / 488·47	3,557 / 7,843	301 / 187	3,000 / 9,845	7,300 / 23,950	1,100 / 683	
Ar 195 V3	1 × 830 hp BMW 132M	2	12·50 / 41 0·1	10·50 / 34 5·4	46·00 / 495·14	3,670 / 8,091	290 / 180	2,000 / 6,560	6,000 / 19,685	650 / 404	
Ar 197 V3	1 × 880 hp BMW 132Dc	1	11·00 / 36 1·1	9·20 / 30 2·2	27·80 / 299·24	2,475 / 5,456	400 / 248	2,500 / 8,200	8,600 / 28,215	659 / 409	
Ar 231	1 × 160 hp HM 501	1	10·18 / 33 4·8	7·81 / 25 7·5	15·20 / 163·61	1,050 / 2,315	170 / 106	S/L	3,000 / 9,845	500 / 310	
BV 40A	None	1	7·90 / 25 11·0	5·70 / 18 8·4	8·70 / 93·65	950 / 2,094	553 / 344	5,790 / 19,000	— / —	— / —	Max speed is for Bf 109G towing aircraft.
BV (Ha) 139B	4 × 600 hp Jumo 205C	4	29·50 / 96 9·4	20·07 / 65 10·2	130·00 / 1,399·31	19,000 / 41,888	288 / 179	3,000 / 9,845	5,000 / 16,405	4,950 / 3,075	
BV 142 V2/U1	4 × 880 hp BMW 132H-1	6	29·53 / 96 10·6	20·48 / 67 2·3	130·00 / 1,399·31	16,560 / 36,508	375 / 233	S/L	9,000 / 29,525	3,900 / 2,423	
BV 144	2 × 1,600 hp BMW 801MA	2 + 18–23	27·00 / 88 7·0	21·80 / 71 6·3	88·00 / 947·22	13,000 / 28,660	470 / 292	4,600 / 15,090	9,100 / 29,855	1,550 / 963	
BV 155 V2	1 × 1,610 hp DB 603A	1	20·50 / 67 3·1	12·00 / 39 4·4	39·00 / 419·79	5,625 / 12,401	690 / 429	16,000 / 52,495	16,950 / 55,610	1,500 / 932	
BV 238 V6	6 × 1,900 hp DB 603G	10	60·17 / 197 4·9	43·36 / 142 3·1	360·17 / 3,876·84	90,000 / 198,416	360 / 223	5,000 / 16,405	6,300 / 20,670	7,850 / 4,878	
Bü 181A	1 × 105 hp HM 504	2	10·60 / 34 9·3	7·85 / 25 9·1	13·50 / 145·31	750 / 1,653	215 / 133	S/L	5,000 / 16,405	800 / 497	
DFS 331 V1	None	?	23·00 / 75 3·5	15·81 / 51 10·4	60·00 / 645·83	4,770 / 10,516	330 / 205	S/L	— / —	— / —	Max towing speed 270 km/h (168 mph).
Do 26D-0 (V6)	4 × 880 hp Jumo 205D	4 + 10–12	30·00 / 98 5·1	24·60 / 80 8·5	120·00 / 1,291·67	20,965 / 46,220	324 / 201	2,600 / 8,530	4,500 / 14,765	4,795 / 2,980	
Do 317B	2 × 2,870 hp DB 610A/B	4	26·00 / 85 3·6	16·80 / 55 1·4	85·00 / 914·93	24,000 / 52,911	670 / 416	7,620 / 25,000	10,515 / 34,500	3,600 / 2,237	All data estimated.
Fi 167A-0	1 × 1,100 hp DB 601B	2	13·50 / 44 3·5	11·40 / 37 4·8	45·50 / 489·76	4,850 / 10,692	320 / 199	S/L	7,500 / 24,605	1,300 / 808	
Fl 282B	1 × 160 hp BMW–Bramo Sh 14A	2	11·96* / 39 2·9	6·56 / 21 6·3	119·00* / 1,280·90	1,000 / 2,205	150 / 93	S/L	3,300 / 10,825	180 / 112	*Rotor diameter and disc area.
Fa 223E	1 × 1,000 hp BMW–Bramo 323Q-3	6	12·00* / 39 4·4	12·25 / 40 2·3	226·00* / 2,432·64	4,315 / 9,513	176 / 109	S/L	4,880 / 16,010	700 / 435	*Rotor diameter and disc area.

Type	Accom.	Power Plant	Span (m / ft in)	Length (m / ft in)	Wing area (m² / sq ft)	Weight (kg / lb)	Max speed (km/h / mph)	at height (m / ft)	Ceiling (m / ft)	Range (km / miles)	Remarks
Fa 330	1	None	7·31* / 24 0·0	4·42 / 14 6·0	41·85* / 450·47	148‡ / 326	40 / 25	S/L	— / —	— / —	* disc area. ‡Empty weight 81 kg (178·5 lb).
Fw 44C	2	1 × 150 hp Sh 14A	9·00 / 29 6·3	7·28 / 23 10·6	20·20 / 217·43	800 / 1,764	190 / 118	S/L	4,400 / 14,430	540 / 335	
Fw 57 V1	3	2 × 910 hp DB 600	25·00 / 82 0·3	16·40 / 53 9·7	73·50 / 791·15	8,300 / 18,298	405 / 252	3,000 / 9,845	9,100 / 29,855	— / —	
Fw 191B	4	2 × 2,870 hp DB 610A/B	26·00 / 85 3·6	19·63 / 64 4·8	70·50 / 758·85	23,860 / 52,602	632 / 393	—	8,775 / 28,790	3,850 / 2,392	All data estimated.
Go 145A	2	1 × 240 hp As 10C	9·00 / 29 6·3	8·70 / 28 6·5	21·75 / 234·11	1,380 / 3,042	212 / 132	S/L	3,700 / 12,140	630 / 391	
He 46C	2	1 × 650 hp Bramo 322B	14·00 / 45 11·2	9·50 / 31 2·0	32·90 / 354·13	2,300 / 5,071	260 / 162	800 / 2,625	6,000 / 19,685	990 / 615	
He 51B-1	1	1 × 750 hp BMW VI 7·3Z	11·00 / 36 1·1	8·40 / 27 6·7	27·20 / 292·78	1,900 / 4,189	330 / 205	S/L	7,700 / 25,260	570 / 354	
He 114A-2	2	1 × 960 hp BMW 132K	13·60 / 44 7·4	11·65 / 38 2·7	42·30 / 455·31	3,670 / 8,091	335 / 208	1,000 / 3,280	4,900 / 16,075	920 / 572	* Estimated.
Hs 124 V2	3	2 × 880 hp BMW 132Dc	18·20 / 59 8·5	14·50 / 47 6·9	54·60 / 587·71	7,230 / 15,939	435 / 270	3,000 / 9,845	6,000* / 19,685	4,200* / 2,610	
Hs 128 V1	2	2 × 1,000 hp DB 601	26·02 / 85 4·4	14·77 / 48 5·5	85·00 / 914·93	— / —	—	—	12,000 / 39,370	— / —	Ceiling is height attained in tests.
Hs 130E-0	3	2 × 1,750 hp DB 603B	33·00 / 108 3·2	22·00 / 72 2·1	— / —	16,700 / 36,817	610 / 379	14,000 / 45,930	15,100 / 49,540	3,000 / 1,864	
Hs 132A	1	1 × 800 kg (1,764 lb) st BMW 003A-1	7·18 / 23 6·7	8·90 / 29 2·4	14·80 / 159·31	3,400 / 7,496	780 / 485	6,000 / 19,685	10,500 / 34,450	1,120 / 696	Performance estimated.
Ju W 33	2 + 6	1 × 310 hp Junkers-L5	18·48 / 60 7·6	10·60 / 34 9·3	44·00 / 473·61	2,700 / 5,952	198 / 123	S/L	4,300 / 14,110	1,000 / 621	
Ju W 34hi	2 + 6	1 × 660 hp BMW 132A	18·48 / 60 7·6	10·27 / 33 8·3	44·00 / 473·61	3,200 / 7,055	265 / 165	S/L	6,300 / 20,670	900 / 559	
Ju G 38	7 + 34	4 × 750 hp Jumo 204	44·00 / 144 4·3	23·20 / 76 1·4	300·00 / 3,229·17	24,000 / 52,911	208* / 129	300 / 985	3,700 / 12,140	1,200 / 746	*Cruising speed.
Ju 252A-1	3 + 32	3 × 1,340 hp Jumo 211F	34·09 / 111 10·1	25·10 / 82 4·2	122·60 / 1,319·65	22,480 / 49,560	439 / 273	5,800 / 19,030	6,300 / 20,670	6,600 / 4,101	
Ju 288C-1	4	2 × 2,950 hp DB 610A-1/B-1	22·657 / 74 4·0	18·15 / 59 6·6	64·70 / 696·42	21,375 / 47,124	655 / 407	6,800 / 22,310	10,400 / 34,120	2,600 / 1,616	Weights and performance estimated.
Ju 352A-1	4 + 32	3 × 1,000/1,200 hp BMW-Bramo 323R-2	34·20 / 112 2·5	24·60 / 80 8·5	128·20 / 1,379·93	19,595 / 43,200	370 / 230	5,050 / 16,570	6,000 / 19,685	2,990 / 1,858	All data estimated.
Ju 488 (V 403)	3	4 × 2,500 hp Jumo 222A-3/B-3	31·28 / 102 7·5	23·24 / 76 3·0	88·00 / 947·22	36,000 / 79,366	690 / 429	7,200 / 23,620	11,350 / 37,240	3,400 / 2,113	
Kl 35D	2	1 × 80 hp HM 508F	10·40 / 34 1·4	7·50 / 24 7·3	15·20 / 163·61	750 / 1,653	212 / 132	S/L	4,350 / 14,270	665 / 413	
Bf 162 V2	3	2 × 986 hp DB 600Aa	17·16 / 56 3·6	12·75 / 41 10·0	— / —	5,800 / 12,787	480 / 298	3,400 / 11,155	— / —	780 / 485	
Me 261 V3	7	2 × 2,950 hp DB610A-1/B-1	26·87 / 88 1·9	16·69 / 54 9·1	76·00* / 818·06	— / —	620 / 385	3,000 / 9,845	8,250 / 27,065	11,000 / 6,835	* Estimated.
Me 309 V4	1	1 × 1,475 hp DB 605B	11·00 / 36 1·1	9·93 / 32 6·9	16·48 / 177·39	4,870 / 10,736	580 / 360	2,200 / 7,220	11,400 / 37,400	1,100 / 683	
Me 328B-1	2	2 × 300 kg (661 lb) st As 014	8·60 / 28 2·6	6·83 / 22 4·9	9·40 / 101·18	3,230 / 7,121	698 / 434	S/L	4,000 / 13,125	750 / 466	

MAJOR LUFTWAFFE WARTIME UNITS AND THEIR PRINCIPAL EQUIPMENT

The following list includes the principal basic Luftwaffe units of World War 2, and the chief types of aircraft used. It should be noted, however, that a particular type did not necessarily form the *only* equipment of any unit at any one time, nor did it necessarily equip all formations of that unit. Often, one Gruppe of a Geschwader, or even one Staffel within a Gruppe, might represent the only formation using a particular type at any given time; space precludes a more detailed list from being given here. Also, it should be remembered that unit titles were frequently changed: KGzbV 1, for example, was later redesignated TG1, and thus the Ju 52/3m is shown against both unit designations. Finally, the entries are of course alphabetical, and not in order of appearance in service.

No fighter was more numerous in the Jagdgeschwadern than the Bf 109; this is a 109E of 7./JG 51

JAGD- und NACHTJAGDVERBÄNDE (Fighter and Night Fighter Units)

Jagdgeschwader 1 Fw 190, He 162, Bf 109.

Jagdgeschwader 2 'Richthofen' Fw 190, Bf 109.

Jagdgeschwader 3 'Udet' Fw 190, Bf 109.

Jagdgeschwader 4 Fw 190, Bf 109.

Jagdgeschwader 5 'Eismeer' Ar 240, Fw 190, Bf 109.

Jagdgeschwader 6 Fw 190, Bf 109.

Jagdgeschwader 7 Bf 109, Me 262.

Jagdgruppe 10 Fw 190, He 177.

Jagdgeschwader 11 Fw 190, Bf 109.

Jagdgeschwader 20 Bf 109.

Jagdgeschwader 21 Bf 109.

Jagdgruppe 25 Bf 109.

Jagdgeschwader 26 'Schlageter' Fw 190, Bf 109.

Jagdgeschwader 27 Bf 109.

An example of Hitler's 'last-ditch' attempts to re-equip Luftwaffe squadrons with jet fighters: a Heinkel He 162A-2 of 3./JG 1

Jagdverbänd 44 Me 262.	**Jagdgeschwader 301** Fw 190, Ta 152, Bf 109.
Jagdgruppe 50 Bf 109.	
Jagdgeschwader 51 'Mölders' Fw 190, Hs 129, Bf 109.	**Jagdgeschwader 302** Fw 190, Bf 109.
Jagdgeschwader 52 Fw 190, Bf 109.	**Jagdgeschwader 400** Me 163.
Jagdgeschwader 53 'Pik-As' Bf 109.	**Ergänzungs Jagdgeschwader 1** Ar 96, Me 163.
Jagdgeschwader 54 'Grünherz' Fw 190, Bf 109.	**Ergänzungs Jagdgeschwader 2** Ar 96, Me 262.
Jagdgeschwader 70 Bf 109.	**Ergänzungs Jagdgeschwader 3** Ar 96.
Jagdgeschwader 71 Bf 109.	**(N) Jagdgeschwader 53** Ar 68.
Jagdgeschwader 76 Bf 109.	**(N) Jagdgeschwader 72** Ar 68.
Jagdgeschwader 77 Bf 109.	**Nachtjagddivision (Holland)** Do 17.
Jagdgeschwader 84 He 162.	**Nachtjagdgeschwader 1** Do 17, Do 215, Do 217, Fw 190, He 219, Ju 88, Bf 109, Bf 110, Me 410.
Jagdgruppe 200 Fw 190, Bf 109.	
Jagdgeschwader 300 Fw 190, Bf 109.	

A Messerschmitt Bf 110G-4a/R2 of 9./NJG 3 (D5 + LT), with Lichtenstein C-1 radar

Nachtjagdgeschwader 2 Do 17, Do 215, Do 217, Ju 88, Bf 110.

Nachtjagdgeschwader 3 Ta 154, Ju 88, Bf 110.

Nachtjagdgeschwader 4 Do 217, Ju 88, Bf 110.

Nachtjagdgeschwader 5 Do 217, He 219, Ju 88, Bf 110, Me 410.

Nachtjagdgeschwader 6 Do 217, Ju 88, Bf 110.

Nachtjagdgruppe 7 Ju 88.

Nachtjagdgruppe 10 Ta 154, He 219, Ju 88, Bf 109, Bf 110.

Nachtjagdgruppe 11 Ju 88, Bf 109, Me 262.

Nachtjagdgeschwader 100 Do 217, Fw 189, Ju 88, Bf 109.

Nachtjagdgeschwader 101 Ju 88.

Nachtjagdgeschwader 102 Ju 88.

Nachtjagdgeschwader 200 Ju 88, Bf 110.

Nachtjagdstaffel Nantes Bf 110.

Nachtjagdstaffel Norwegen He 219, Ju 88, Bf 110.

Messerschmitt's Me 410 finally provided a viable Zerstörer successor to the Bf 110 after the failure of the Me 210

ZERSTÖRERVERBÄNDE (Long-Range Fighter Units)

Zerstörergeschwader 1 'Wespen' Ju 88, Bf 109, Bf 110, Me 210, Me 410.

Zerstörergeschwader 2 Bf 109, Bf 110.

Zerstörergeschwader 26 'Horst Wessel' Ju 88, Bf 109, Bf 110, Me 210, Me 410.

Zerstörergeschwader 52 Bf 109, Bf 110.

Zerstörergeschwader 76 Bf 109, Bf 110, Me 410.

6., 7. and 10. Staffeln (Z)/Jagdgeschwader 5 Bf 110.

13. Staffel (Z)/Jagdgeschwader 5 Ar 240, Bf 110.

13. Staffel (Z)/Jagdgeschwader 77 Fw 187.

KAMPFVERBÄNDE (Bomber Units)

Kampfgeschwader 1 'Hindenburg' He 111, He 177, Ju 88.

Kampfgeschwader 2 'Holzhammer' Do 17, Do 217, Ju 88, Ju 188, Me 410.

Kampfgeschwader 3 'Blitz' Do 17, Fi 103, He 111, Ju 88.

Kampfgeschwader 4 'General Wever' He 111, He 177, Ju 88.

Kampfgeschwader 6 Do 217, He 111, Ju 86, Ju 88, Ju 188, Bf 109, Me 210.

Kampfgeschwader 25 Ju 88.

Kampfgeschwader 26 'Löwen'   He III, He 177, Ju 88, Ju 188.

Kampfgeschwader 27 'Boelcke'   He III, Ju 88.

Kampfgeschwader 28   He III, Ju 88.

Kampfgeschwader 30 'Adler'   Ju 88.

Kampfgeschwader 40   Do 217, Fw 200, He III, He 177, Hs 293, Ju 88.

Kampfgeschwader 50   He 177.

Kampfgeschwader 51 'Edelweiss'   Do 17, Fw 190, He III, Ju 88, Me 262, Me 410.

Kampfgeschwader 53 'Legion Condor'   Do 17, Fi 103, He III.

Kampfgeschwader 54 'Totenkopf'   He III, Ju 88, Me 262.

Kampfgeschwader 55 'Griefen'   He III, Ju 88, Bf 109, Bf 110.

Kampfgeschwader 60   Ju 88.

Kampfgeschwader 66   Do 217, Ju 88, Ju 188.

Kampfgeschwader 76   Ar 234, Do 17, Ju 88.

Kampfgeschwader 77   Do 17, Ju 88.

Kampfgeschwader 100   Ar 196, Do 17, Do 217, Fw 200, He III, He 177, Hs 293, Ju 88.

Kampfgeschwader 101   Do 217, Ju 88.

Kampfgruppe 106   Ju 88.

Kampfgruppe 126   He III.

Kampfgeschwader 200   Ar 196, Ar 232, Do 217, Fi 103R, Fw 190, Fw 200, Go 242, He 59, He III, He 115, He 177, Hs 126, Hs 293, Ju 88, Ju 188, Ju 252, Ju 290, Ju 352, Bf 109.

Kampfgruppe 506   Ju 88.

Kampfgruppe 606   Do 17, Ju 88.

Kampfgruppe 806   He III, Ju 88.

Schnellkampfgeschwader 210   Fw 190, Bf 109, Bf 110.

Backbone of the Kampfgeschwadern throughout the war was the Heinkel He III

Although primarily a ground attack type, this Hs 123A bears the 'S4' code of Kü Fl Gr 506 and the badge of FFS A/B 113

SCHLACHT- und STUKAVERBÄNDE
(Close Support and Dive-Bomber Units)

Nachtschlachtgruppe 1 Ju 87.	Go 145, He 46,	**Schlachtgeschwader 2** Hs 129, Ju 87, Bf 109.	Fw 190, Hs 123,
Nachtschlachtgruppe 2 87.	Ar 66, Go 145, Ju	**Schlachtgeschwader 3**	Fw 190, Ju 87.
Nachtschlachtgruppe 3	Ar 66, Go 145.	**Schlachtgeschwader 4**	Fw 190.
Nachtschlachtgruppe 4 87.	Ar 66, Go 145, Ju	**Schlachtgeschwader 5**	Fw 190, Ju 87.
Nachtschlachtgruppe 5	Ar 66, Go 145.	**Schlachtgeschwader 9**	Fw 190, Hs 129.
Nachtschlachtgruppe 6	Go 145.	**Schlachtgeschwader 10**	Fw 190.
Nachtschlachtgruppe 7	Hs 126.	**Schlachtgeschwader 77**	Fw 190, Ju 87.
Nachtschlachtgruppe 8	Ar 66.	**Schlachtgeschwader 101**	Hs 129.
Nachtschlachtgruppe 9	Fw 190, Ju 87.	**Störkampfstaffeln** W 34.	Ar 66, Go 145, Ju
Nachtschlachtgruppe 10	Ju 87.	**Stukageschwader 1**	Do 17, Ju 87, Bf 110.
Nachtschlachtgruppe 11	Ar 66, Hs 126.	**Stukageschwader 2** Bf 110.	Do 17, Hs 123, Ju 87,
Nachtschlachtgruppe 12	Ar 66, Hs 126.	**Stukageschwader 3**	Do 17, Ju 87, Bf 110.
Nachtschlachtgruppe 20	Fw 190.	**Stukageschwader 5**	Ju 87.
Nachtschlachtgruppe 30	Ju 88.	**Stukageschwader 51**	Do 17, Ju 87.
Schlachtgeschwader 1 Hs 129, Ju 87, Bf 109.	Fw 190, Hs 123,	**Stukageschwader 76**	Do 17, Ju 87.
		Stukageschwader 77	Do 17, Ju 87, Bf 110.

AUFKLÄRUNGSVERBÄNDE (Reconnaissance Units)

Aufklärungsgruppe Oberbefehlshaber der Luftwaffe   Ar 240, Ha 142, Do 215, Do 217, He 111, Ju 86, Ju 88, Bf 109, Bf 110, Me 261.

Aufklärungsgruppe 10 'Tannenberg'   Ar 240, Do 17, Fw 189, Hs 126, Ju 88, Bf 110.

Aufklärungsgruppe 11   Do 17, Do 217, Fw 189, He 46, Hs 126, Ju 88, Ju 188, Bf 110.

Aufklärungsgruppe 12   Fw 189, He 46, Hs 126, Bf 109, Bf 110.

Aufklärungsgruppe 13   Do 17, Fw 189, He 46, Hs 126, Bf 109, Bf 110.

Aufklärungsgruppe 14   Do 17, Fi 156, Fw 189, He 46, Hs 126, Ju 88, Ju 188, Bf 109, Bf 110.

Aufklärungsgruppe 21   Fi 156, Fw 189, Hs 126, Bf 109.

Aufklärungsgruppe 22   Do 17, Hs 126, Ju 88, Ju 188, Bf 110, Me 410.

Aufklärungsgruppe 23   He 46, Hs 126.

Aufklärungsgruppe 31   Do 17, Fw 189, He 46, Hs 126, Bf 110.

Aufklärungsgruppe 32   Fw 189, Fw 190, Hs 126, Bf 109.

Aufklärungsgruppe 33   Ar 234, Ju 88, Ju 188, Bf 109, Bf 110, Me 410.

Aufklärungsgruppe 41   Fw 189, Hs 126.

Aufklärungsgruppe 100   Ar 234, Ar 240, Do 215, Ju 86, Ju 88, Ju 188, Bf 109.

Aufklärungsgruppe 120   Do 17, Fw 200, He 111, Ju 88, Ju 188, Bf 109.

Aufklärungsgruppe 121   Do 17, Fw 190, He 111, Ju 88, Ju 188, Bf 109, Bf 110, Me 410.

Aufklärungsgruppe 122   Ar 240, Do 17, Fw 190, Fw 200, He 111, Ju 88, Ju 188, Bf 109, Bf 110, Me 210, Me 410.

Aufklärungsgruppe 123   Ar 234, Ar 240, Do 17, Do 217, Fw 190, He 111, Ju 86, Ju 88, Ju 188, Bf 109, Bf 110.

Aufklärungsgruppe 124   Do 17, Do 215, He 111, Ju 88, Ju 188, Bf 109, Bf 110.

Aufklärungsgruppe 156   Fi 156.

Aufklärungsgruppe Nacht and Nachtaufklärungsstaffeln   Do 17, Do 215, Do 217, Fw 189, He 111, Hs 126, Ju 88, Ju 188, Bf 109, Bf 110.

Aufklarungsstaffel (See) 222   BV 222.

Fernaufklärungsgruppe 1   Ju 188, Me 410.

Fernaufklärungsgruppe 2   Ju 188.

Fernaufklärungsgruppe 3   Ju 188, Me 410.

Fernaufklärungsgruppe 5   Do 217, Ju 290, Ju 390.

Nahaufklärungsgruppe 1   Fw 189, Hs 126, Bf 109, Bf 110.

Nahaufklärungsgruppe 2   Fw 189, Fw 190, Hs 126, Bf 109.

One of the standard types of reconnaissance aircraft flown by the Aufklärungsverbände: the Focke-Wulf Fw 189

Nahaufklärungsgruppe 3 126, Bf 109.	Fw 189, Hs	Nahaufklärungsgruppe 15 109, Bf 110.	Fw 189, Bf
Nahaufklärungsgruppe 4 126, Bf 109.	Fw 189, Hs	Nahaufklärungsgruppe 16 110.	Fw 189, Bf
Nahaufklärungsgruppe 5 Bf 110.	Hs 126, Bf 109,	Seeaufklärungsgruppe 125 196, BV 138, He 60, He 114.	Ar 95, Ar
Nahaufklärungsgruppe 6 262.	Bf 110, Me	Seeaufklärungsgruppe 126 196, BV 138, He 60, He 114.	Ar 95, Ar
Nahaufklärungsgruppe 7	Hs 126.	Seeaufklärungsgruppe 127 196, He 60, Hs 126.	Ar 95, Ar
Nahaufklärungsgruppe 8 126, Bf 109, Bf 110.	Fw 189, Hs	Seeaufklärungsgruppe 128	Ar 196.
Nahaufklärungsgruppe 9 109.	Fw 189, Bf	Seeaufklärungsgruppe 129 222.	BV 138, BV
Nahaufklärungsgruppe 10 126, Bf 109.	Fw 189, Hs	Seeaufklärungsgruppe 130 138, BV 222.	Ar 196, BV
Nahaufklärungsgruppe 11 190, Hs 126, Bf 109.	Fw 189, Fw	Seeaufklärungsgruppe 131 138, BV 222.	Ar 196, BV
Nahaufklärungsgruppe 12 126, Ju 88, Bf 109.	Fw 189, Hs	Seeaufklärungsgruppe 132 138.	Ar 196, BV
Nahaufklärungsgruppe 13 190, Bf 109, Bf 110.	Fw 189, Fw	Sonder-Aufklärungsstaffel Oberbefehlshaber der Luftwaffe 240, Ju 188.	Ar
Nahaufklärungsgruppe 14 189, Bf 109, Bf 110.	Fi 156, Fw		

TRANSPORTVERBÄNDE (Transport Units)

Fliegerführer-Transportstaffeln   Ju
W 34.
Führerkurierstaffel   Fw 200, Ju 290.
Go 242 Staffeln   Go 242.

**Grossraumlastenseglergruppe Me
321**   Me 321.
**Grossraumlastensegler-Kommando
2**   Me 321.

A Gotha Go 242 transport glider with cargo and raised rear fuselage

A 'Tante Ju' (Ju 52/3m) of III./TG 3, en route for Norway

Ju 352 Gruppe   Ju 352.
Kampfgeschwadern (und Kampfgruppen)
zbV 1, 2, 3, 6, 7, 8, 9, 11, 12, 40, 50, 60, 101,
102, 103, 107, 172, 300, 400, 500, 600, 700, 800,
900, 999, Brindisi, Frankfurt, Naples, Oels
Posen, Reggio and Wittstock   Ju 52/3m.
Kampfgruppe zbV 4   Ju W 34.
Kampfgruppe zbV 5   Go 242, He 111, Ju
52/3m.
Kampfgruppen zbV 20, 23 and 25   He
111.
Kampfgruppen zbV 21 and 22   Ju 86.
Kampfgruppe zbV 30   Go 242, He 111.
Kampfgruppen zbV 104 and 106   Go 244,
Ju 52/3m.
Kampfgruppe zbV 105   Ha 142, Fw 200,
Ju 52/3m.
Kampfgruppe zbV 108 See   BV 138, Ha
139, Do 24, He 59, Ju 52/3m.
Kampfgruppe zbV 200   Fw 200.
Kampfgruppe zbV 323   Me 323.
Lastenseglerstaffeln   DFS 230.
Luftlandegeschwader 1   Do 17, DFS 230,
Go 242, He 111, Hs 126.
Luftlandegeschwader 2   DFS 230, Go
242.
Luft-Transportgeschwader See   BV 138,
Ha 139, Do 24, Do 26, He 59, Ju W 33, Ju G 38.
Luft-Transportstaffel 40   Fl 282, Fa 223.

Luft-Transportstaffel (See) 222   BV 222.
Luft-Transportstaffel 290   Fw 200, Ju 90,
Ju 252, Ju 290.
Luftverkehrsgesellschaft Bronkow   Ju
52/3m.
Luftverkehrsgesellschaft Mobil   Ju
52/3m.
Schleppgruppe 1   DFS 230, Go 242, He
111.
Schleppgruppe 2   DFS 230, Go 242.
Schleppgruppe 3   DFS 230, Go 242.
Schleppgruppe 4   Go 242, He 111.
Seetransportstaffeln 1 and 2   Do 24, Ju
52/3m.
Transportfliegerstaffel Condor   Fw 200.
Transportgeschwader 1   Ju 52/3m.
Transportgeschwader 2   Ju 52/3m.
Transportgeschwader 3   Go 244, He 111,
Ju 52/3m.
Transportgeschwader 4   Ar 232, Go 244,
Ju 52/3m.
Transportgeschwader 5   Ar 232, Ju
52/3m, Me 323.
Transportgruppe 20   Ju 52/3m.
Transportgruppe 30   He 111, Ju 52/3m.
Transportgruppe 111   He 111.
Transportstaffel 5   Ar 232, Ju 90, Ju 252,
Ju 290, Me 264.
Transportstaffel 200   Fw 200.

The He 115 was used widely by the maritime patrol and reconnaissance units. This He 115B-1/R2 is being loaded with a practice torpedo

SEE- und KÜSTENFLIEGERVERBÄNDE (Maritime Units)

Bordfliegergruppe 196   Ar 196, BV 138, He 114.

Küstenfliegergruppe 106   Do 18, He 59, He 60, He 115.

Küstenfliegergruppe 206   He 60.

Küstenfliegergruppe 306   He 60.

Küstenfliegergruppe 406   BV 138, Ha 139, BV 222, Do 18, Do 26, He 59, He 60, He 115.

Küstenfliegergruppe 506   BV 138, Do 18, Do 26, He 59, He 60, He 114, He 115.

Küstenfliegergruppe 606   He 115.

Küstenfliegergruppe 706   Ar 196, BV 138, He 59, He 115.

Küstenfliegergruppe 806   Do 18, He 60.

Küstenfliegergruppe 906   BV 138, Do 18, He 115.

Küstenstaffel 'Krim'   Bf 110.

Minensuchgruppe 1 der Luftwaffe   BV 138, Ju 52/3m.

Seenotkommando Varna   Do 24.

Seenotstaffeln   Do 24, He 59.

Sonderstaffel 'Tranz-Ozean'   Ha 139.

Trägergruppe 186   Ju 87, Bf 109.

TRAINING AND MISCELLANEOUS OTHER UNITS

Einsatzkommando Braunegg   Me 262.

Einsatzkommando Schenk   Me 262.

Erprobungsgruppe 210   Bf 109, Bf 110, Me 210.

Erprobungsgruppe Kopenhagen   Bf 110.

Erprobungskommando 16   Me 163.

Erprobungskommando 17   He 111.

Erprobungskommando 25   He 177, Bf 109, Me 410.

Erprobungskommando 26   Hs 129.

Erprobungskommando 40   Fw 58.

Erprobungskommando 88   Ju 88.

Two examples of the Ar 96B, one of the Luftwaffe's chief wartime training aircraft

Erprobungskommando 152	Ta 152.	
Erprobungskommando 162	He 162.	
Erprobungskommando 188	Ju 188.	
Erprobungskommando 262	Me 262.	
Erprobungskommando 335	Do 335.	
Erprobungskommando 388	Ju 388.	
Erprobungsstaffel 167	Fi 167.	

Fliegergruppe-Ost Ar 66, Go 145.

Flugzeugführerschulen Ar 66, Ar 96, Ju W 33, Ju W 34, Kl 35.

Jagdfliegerschulen Fw 56.

Jagdschulgeschwadern Ar 96.

Kommando Bonow Ar 234.

Kommando Edelweiss Me 262.

Kommando Götz Ar 234.

Kommando Hecht Ar 234.

Kommando Koch He 111.*

Kommando Kunkel Bf 110.

Kommando Nowotny Me 262.

Kommando Sperling Ar 234.

Kommando Stamp Me 262.

Kommando Welter Me 262.

Lehrgeschwader 1 He 111, Ju 87, Ju 88, Bf 110.

Lehrgeschwader 2 Do 17, Fw 189, Fw 190, Hs 123, Hs 126, Hs 129, Bf 109, Bf 110.

Lehr- und Erprobungskommando 21 Do 217.

Lehr- und Erprobungskommando 36 He 111, He 177, Hs 293.

Lehr- und Erprobungskommando 100 He 111.

Luftkriegsschulen Ar 96.

Panzerjägerstaffel 92 Ju 88.

Rammkommando Elbe Bf 109.

Sonderkommando 9 Fw 56.

Versuchsstaffel 210 Me 210.

Versuchsverbänd Oberbefehlshaber der Luftwaffe Ar 234, Ar 240, Ju 86, Ju 88, Ju 188, Ju 388, Bf 109, Me 262.

Wettererkundungsstaffeln Ar 232, He 111, He 177, Ju 88, Bf 110.

Wüstennotstaffeln Fi 156.

Zerstörerschulen Bf 109, Bf 110.

PRINCIPAL GERMAN AERO-ENGINES 1939–1945

PISTON ENGINES

	Cylinders	Arrangement	Cooling		Cylinders	Arrangement	Cooling
Argus As 10	8	IV	A	Hirth HM 501	6	IIL	A
As 410	12	IV	A	HM 504	4	IIL	A
As 411	12	IV	A	HM 508	8	IV	A
BMW VI	12	V	L	Junkers Jumo 205	6	VO	L
132	9	R	A	Jumo 207	6	VO	L
801	14	R	A	Jumo 210	12	IV	L
BMW-Bramo 314	7	R	A	Jumo 211	12	IV	L
322	9	R	A	Jumo 213	12	IV	L
323 Fafnir	9	R	A	Jumo 222	24	R	L
Daimler-Benz DB 600	12	IV	L				
DB 601	12	IV	L				
DB 603	12	IV	L				
DB 605	12	IV	L				
DB 606	24	IV	L				
DB 610	24	IV	L	(A: air-cooled; L: liquid-cooled; V: Vee; IV:			
DB 627	12	IV	L	inverted Vee; IIL: inverted in-line; R: radial;			
				VO: vertically-opposed)			

JET AND ROCKET ENGINES

	Type		Type
Argus As 014	Pulse-jet	Heinkel-Hirth 011 (HeS 11)	Axial turbojet
As 044	Pulse-jet	Junkers Jumo 004 Orkan	Axial turbojet
BMW 003 Sturm	Axial turbojet	012	Axial turbojet
Daimler-Benz 007	Axial turbojet	Walter HWK 509	Liquid-fuel
Heinkel HeS 1, 3, 8, 10	Axial turbojets		rocket

ABBREVIATIONS

BFGr Bordfliegergruppe (Shipboard Aviation Group).

BFW Bayerische Flugzeugwerke AG.

BK Bordkanone (fixed aircraft cannon).

BMW Bayerische Motorenwerke GmbH.

DB Daimler-Benz AG.

DFS Deutsches Forschungsinstitut für Segelflug (German Gliding Research Institute).

DLH Deutsche Luft Hansa.

DLV Deutscher Luftsportverbänd (German Aviation Sport Union).

DVL Deutsche Versuchsanstalt für Luftfahrt (German Aviation Experimental Establishment).

EJG Ergänzungs-Jagdgeschwader (Fighter Replacement Training Wing).

EK or **EKdo** Erprobungskommando (Testing Detachment).

FAGr Fernaufklärungsgruppe (Long Range Reconnaissance Group).

FFS Flugzeugführerschule (Pilot School).

FuG Funkgerät (radio or radar equipment).

FZG Fernzielgerät (remote aiming device) or Flakzielgerät (anti-aircraft aiming device).

HFB Hamburger Flugzeugbau GmbH.

HWK Hellmuth Walter KG.

JFS Jagdfliegerschule (Fighter Pilot School).

JG Jagdgeschwader (Fighter Wing).

JSG Jagdschulgeschwader (Fighter Training Wing).

KG Kampfgeschwader (Battle Wing).

KGzbV Kampfgeschwader zur besonderen Verwendung (Battle Wing for Special Duties).

Kü Fl Gr Küstenfliegergruppe (Coastal Aviation Group).

LKS   Luftkriegsschule (Air Warfare School).

LTS   Luft-Transportstaffel (Air Transport Squadron).

MG   Maschinengewehr (machine-gun), as in MG 17.

MK   Maschinenkanone (machine-cannon), as in MK 108.

NAGr   Nahaufklärungsgruppe (Short Range Reconnaissance Group).

NJG   Nachtjagdgeschwader (Night Fighter Wing).

NSFK   Nationalsozialistischen Fliegerkorps (National Socialist Aviation Corps).

NSGr   Nachtschlachtgruppe (Night Harassment Group).

Ob d L   Oberbefehlshaber der Luftwaffe (Commander-in-Chief of the Luftwaffe).

OKL   Oberkommando der Luftwaffe (High Command of the Luftwaffe).

Pz   Panzer (tank or armour).

R   Rüstsatz (field conversion kit), as in He 219A-5/R1.

RLM   Reichsluftfahrtministerium (German Aviation Ministry).

SAGr   Seeaufklärungsgruppe (Maritime Reconnaissance Group).

SG or **Sch G**   Schlachtgeschwader (Harassment or Assault Wing).

St G   Sturzkampfgeschwader or Stukageschwader (Dive Bomber Wing).

U   Umrüst-Bausatz (factory conversion kit), as in Me 410A-2/U4.

V   Versuchs (Experimental or Prototype), as in Bf 110 V1, Fw 190 V21.

W Gr or **Wfr Gr**   Werfer-Granate (rocket-propelled shell), as in W Gr 21.

WNF   Wiener-Neustädter Flugzeugwerke GmbH.

ZG   Zerstörergeschwader (Destroyer or 'Heavy Fighter' Wing).

APPENDIX 6

SELECTED BIBLIOGRAPHY

GREEN, W. *Rocket Fighter*. (Purnell, London 1970.)

GREEN, W. *Warplanes of the Third Reich*. (Macdonald, London 1970.)

GUNSTON, B. *The Encyclopedia of the World's Combat Aircraft*. (Hamlyn/Salamander, London 1976.)

MUNSON, K. *Bombers, Patrol and Transport Aircraft 1939–1945*. (Blandford Press, London 1969.)

MUNSON, K. *Fighters, Attack and Training Aircraft 1939–1945*. (Blandford Press, London 1969.)

NOWARRA, H. J., and KENS, K-H. *Die deutschen Flugzeuge 1933–1945*. (J. F. Lehmanns Verlag, München 1968.)

PRICE, A. *Battle Over the Reich*. (Ian Allan, Shepperton 1963.)

RIES, K. *Luftwaffen-Story 1935–1939*. (Verlag Dieter Hoffmann, Mainz 1974.)

RIES, K. *Markings and Camouflage Systems of Luftwaffe Aircraft in World War II, Vols I to IV*. (Verlag Dieter Hoffmann, Mainz 1963–1972.)

SMITH, J. R., and KAY, A. *German Aircraft of the Second World War*. (Putnam, London 1972.)

TAYLOR, J. W. R. (Ed.) *Combat Aircraft of the World*. (Ebury Press and Michael Joseph, London 1969.)

WEAL, E. C. and J. A. *Combat Aircraft of World War Two*. (Arms and Armour Press, London 1977.)

INDEX
(Main references in bold type)